Praise for
Raising the Kid You Love with The Ex You Hate

"If you are divorced, or contemplating divorce, you need this book. Drawing on decades of experience helping families, Dr. Farber's time-tested advice shows parents how to do right by their children. With clarity and compassion, the book helps parents anticipate and avoid common pitfalls. Follow Dr. Farber's wise and practical rules and your children will flourish after the breakup, secure in the knowledge that your love for them trumps your disappointments in the marriage."

—Dr. Richard A. Warshak, clinical professor at The University of Texas Southwestern Medical Center and author of *Divorce Poison: How To Protect Your Family From Bad-mouthing and Brainwashing and Welcome Back, Pluto: Understanding, Preventing, and Overcoming Parental Alienation*

"Divorce is hard on kids, but what hurts kids even more is nasty conflict between their parents. Based on his extensive experience with children of divorce, clinical psychologist Edward Farber provides an invaluable guide through the minefield of mistakes that angry ex-spouses need to avoid in order to co-parent after a divorce."

—Dianne L. Chambless, PhD, professor and director of clinical psychology training at the University of Pennsylvania

"Dr. Farber's book is a must read for divorcing/divorced parents who want to insure their children's well-being and future adjustment. Dr. Farber adeptly describes the hurt and anger that parents in this difficult life transition can feel and how these negative feelings can cloud parents' decisions about and actions toward the children they love. Using case examples to illustrate the feelings, dilemmas, and decisions that divorcing/divorced parents face, Dr. Farber provides practical child development-enhancing strategies and prescriptions that will guide parents to facilitate their children's emotional sturdiness and well-being over time."

—Dr. Carol Weissbrod, director of clinical training and associate professor of psychology at American University

"Dr. Farber is that 'good conscience' we'd all like to have looking over our shoulders. His light touch and solid practical advice for the divorced parent is easy to read and sure to save readers and their children from a lot of anxiety and legal bills. I can't wait for his next book full of guidance for other aspects of our lives!"

—Dan Oren, MD, psychiatrist and medical director of BH Care and co-author of *How to Beat Jet Lag*

RAISING THE
KID YOU
Love
WITH THE
EX YOU
HATE

RAISING THE
KID YOU
Love
WITH THE
EX YOU
HATE

EDWARD FARBER, PhD

This book is intended as a reference volume only. It is sold with the understanding that the publisher and author are not engaged in rendering any professional services. The information given here is designed to help you make informed decisions. If you suspect that you have a problem that might require professional treatment or advice, you should seek competent help.

Published by River Grove Books
Austin, TX
www.rivergrovebooks.com

Copyright © 2013 Edward Farber

All rights reserved.

Thank you for purchasing an authorized edition of this book and for complying with copyright law. No part of this book may be reproduced, stored in a retrieval system, or transmitted by any means, electronic, mechanical, photocopying, recording, or otherwise, without written permission from the copyright holder.

Distributed by River Grove Books

Design and composition by Greenleaf Book Group
Cover design by Greenleaf Book Group
Cover image ©marish/Veer.

Publisher's Cataloging-in-Publication data is available.

Print ISBN: 978-1-63299-656-5

eBook ISBN: 978-1-60832-421-7

First Edition

*To Pam for her many years of love and support
And to Yoni and Orly*

CONTENTS

Preface xiii
Introduction 1
    When It's All About Hate 4
    Making It Work—for the Child 6
    It Should Be All About Love 8

PART ONE Co-Parenting 101

CHAPTER 1 Congratulations, You Are Divorced—Now Start
Co-Parenting 11
    Co-Parenting Defined: Why It's for You 13
    Rule 1: Your Child Needs Both Parents 16
    Rule 2: Reduce Parental Conflict After the Separation 21
    Rule 3: Both Parents Make Decisions 26

CHAPTER 2 What Your Child Needs to Know—and What
He Doesn't 31
    How Much to Say 34
    When and How to Tell Them 35
    What She Thinks When You Say "Divorce" 37
    Your First Steps as a Co-Parent 40

CHAPTER 3 Money Matters: Child Support Is for the Child 45
    Funding Your Co-Parenting 49

CONTENTS

CHAPTER 4	Together Again—Sort of: From Holidays to Soccer Games	53
	Showing Up at the Games	55
	Sharing the Love—Handling the Holidays	58
	The Middle Ground for Your Child	60
CHAPTER 5	Everyday Matters: School and Religion	65
	Choosing a New School If You Must	68
	New School: Parental Adjustment Required	70
	Matters of Faith	72

PART TWO What If . . . Co-Parenting the Unexpected, and Inevitable

CHAPTER 6	Introducing New People into Your Child's Life	79
	You Love Him, You Love Her: When Should They Meet?	81
	A Stepparent Is Not a Co-Parent	89
CHAPTER 7	Accusations of Abuse or Abusive Accusations?	97
CHAPTER 8	When Your Ex Just Says No	105
	Your Ex Is a Bully	111
CHAPTER 9	The Ex with Psychological Problems	115
	It's Your Ex's Problem, Not Your Child's	121
	Fit to Parent?	122

PART THREE Your Kid Said What?

CHAPTER 10	"Hell No—I Won't Go!": Your Child Refuses Visitation	133
	Giving In Is Not Giving Up	138
	You Are Still the Parent. Act Like One.	141

CHAPTER 11 "She's Moving Out—and In with Him!" 145

　　　　　　　　If You Love Your Child, Let Him Go 152

CHAPTER 12 Don't Believe Everything Your Child Says 155

　　　　　　　　What Your Child Really Wants and Needs 158

PART FOUR **Till Death Do You Co-Parent**

CHAPTER 13 Breaking Up Your Breakup 163

　　　　　　　　Don't Even Think About Co-Parenting When 167

　　　　　　　　Think About Co-Parenting, but... 169

　　　　　　　　Parent Coordination 171

CHAPTER 14 Protecting Your Family Forever 185

　　　　　　　　Letting Go of Anger 187

　　　　　　　　Good Parenting, Even When You Disagree 190

　　　　　　　　A Better Parent After the Divorce 193

　　　　　　　　You Are Still a Family 196

ACKNOWLEDGMENTS 201

INDEX 203

ABOUT THE AUTHOR 211

PREFACE

In the ten years since I wrote *Raising the Kid You Love with the Ex You Hate*, thousands of families have put aside the hurt from their divorce and learned that the mental health and well-being of their child are far more important than the anger toward their ex.

To some parents, the idea that children should have meaningful relationships with both parents after divorce seems preposterous. But having such a relationship, absent of conflict, is best for your child now and in the future. Used by judges, lawyers, psychologists, and therapists, *Raising the Kid You Love with the Ex You Hate* has helped families navigate the process of separation and divorce. A family lawyer ordered over 100 copies and hands them out to each new client. Judges have sent parents arguing about extracurricular activities or medical choices out of the courtroom with orders to read it. Hundreds of mental health professionals have been trained on the principles of effective co-parenting.

Learn to avoid conflict and make co-parenting work for you and your child.

INTRODUCTION

Colin was seven when his parents divorced. He lived with his mother and she made most of the day-to-day decisions, but Colin's father was involved in academic, health, and extracurricular activity decision making. Colin frequently spent time with his father on weekends and knew he was a part of his life.

Father remarried and took a position in California. Once a month, Father would come to DC for work and arranged the trips so he could be in Washington over the weekend. The parents' flexibility allowed him to see Colin weekday evenings when Father was in DC, too. Father always stayed at the same suite-style hotel, and the hotel stored a duffel with some of Colin's clothes, games, books, toys, and pictures to make the suite feel like home. Father would always tack Colin's school projects to the walls, arrange his books and an extra Game Boy around his bed, and place photos of Colin's dog, baseball team, and family vacations in picture frames around the room. Colin had access to a laptop and video games at the hotel.

A few days before Father planned a visit, Mother would email him the title of whatever book Colin was reading, and Father would make sure to get a copy to leave by Colin's bed in the room. Colin only had to add his weekend sports uniforms to the homework in his backpack on the Thursdays and Fridays his father would pick him up from school. Colin could invite friends on the weekend, and, especially during the winter, the hotel's small indoor swimming pool and gym were a hit with his buddies. Teacher meetings and routine pediatrician visits were often arranged during the week of visitation so Father could attend, and during that week Father took over transporting Colin to sports practices, religious school classes, and piano lessons.

Even though parental decision making became more and more Mother's responsibility, Father was involved during his monthly visits. He provided money for Colin's care, and his input was welcome. Parental conflict was kept to a minimum.

The parents agreed that Colin would fly to California several times a year over long weekends and extended school holidays using Father's frequent flyer miles, but the difficulty of transportation quickly became apparent. Colin was anxious both about flying by himself, even as an accompanied minor, and about missing sports and friends over the breaks. Although he enjoyed seeing his father and stepmother, he had no friends in California and was often bored. Transcontinental travel also disrupted Colin's sleep, and Colin would be tired for several days after he came home. Father didn't have a piano, so Colin couldn't practice while there, either.

Then one President's Day weekend, a major storm delayed Colin's plane. His nonstop flight ended up landing in the Midwest and was then diverted away from LAX to an alternate airport in California. After nearly twenty hours of commuting, Colin had had enough, and his parents agreed that short three- and four-day visits to California would end. Instead, Colin would go to California for part of his Christmas holiday, spring breaks, and a month in the summer. Since Colin still didn't have friends in California, his summer visits were arranged so that he could attend local summer camps most of the month. His father even bought an electric keyboard, hoping that Colin could use that to practice the piano over the summer.

The few conflicts the parents had were relatively easily resolved, and Colin didn't display major problems other than some anxieties. He was a somewhat shy, slow-to-warm-up boy, hesitantly adapting to new situations. Father backed off over imposing his feelings about Colin's development, learned how to give his opinions in a non-forceful manner, and honored his financial obligations. Father didn't challenge the cost of orthodontist consults or longer piano lessons. Thanks to their extended monthly visits, Father and Colin had a comfortable, solid relationship, and Father actively participated in his son's growth and development.

When Colin was eleven, his father was promoted to senior management. Along with greater job satisfaction and financial rewards, however, came what others would have seen as a plus, but for Colin's dad was a major negative: He no longer had to travel monthly to Washington. Instead, he now traveled regularly to company headquarters in Seattle. Financially, Father could afford to fly east to see Colin once a month, but now he didn't have the time. Ramped-up job responsibilities meant he couldn't take off during the week; he could fly in only on long weekends. The suite where Father had spent one week a month no longer kept his duffel. Father could no longer be relied upon to drive Colin to practices and religious school once a month. Now too, Colin's stepmother was pregnant, and, for Father, the idea of regularly traveling back east became less and less viable. The arrangement that had been working so well at giving Colin meaningful contact with both parents was now in jeopardy.

When It's All About Hate

Every day in my office I see parents, embittered by divorce and so grateful to finally be physically and legally apart from a partner they once loved and now hate, struggling to co-parent and jointly make decisions about their children.

Every day, adults who once loved each other so much that they promised to stay together until the end of time storm into my office, dragging behind them children dejected and battered by Mom and Dad's rage toward each other.

Day in and day out I find myself saying the same things over and over. "Your child needs a meaningful relationship with both of her parents . . . Control your frustrations and anger and deal with your ex in a businesslike manner . . . Your son needs both of you to make the decisions important for his development."

Your war with your ex is hurting your child more than you can ever imagine—much more than you are hurting each other. You and your ex must learn to work together to raise your child. Think of raising your child like running a business. Business partners don't have to be friends; they may not even like one another. But they know that, for their business to succeed, they must work together and make decisions together. You have a business that produces a priceless product: the child you love, whom you must raise with the ex you hate.

Sometimes my insights help the people in my office. Sadly, sometimes they don't, when warring exes cannot get far enough past the hate they have for each to think first of the child they both love. But more often than not, the angry exes do learn what they must do to raise their child together. Their marriage is at an end, but the child they jointly brought into this world demands that they enter into a new kind of relationship.

I hope that this book can show you how to enter into this new relationship and make life a whole lot better and a whole lot healthier for you and your child.

Ultimately you and your ex have a choice. You can either work together to launch your child into a future filled with promise and potential, or you can continue to fight and squabble, most likely sentencing your child to a future filled with doubts, insecurities, and self-blame—and that's just for starters.

Years ago, I didn't realize the stakes in divorce were so high. As a clinical psychologist I had worked with many children who had suffered terrible traumas. My patients were children who had lost a parent, adolescents with chronic diseases, and young people sexually abused by authority figures whom they had trusted.

When I first started to see children of divorce, I thought their problems would be mild compared to those of my seriously traumatized patients. But over the years I have seen custody battles lead to the most serious of tragedies for the children: from failure at school and chronic illness to drug addiction, debilitating mental challenges, and even murder.

The bottom line is that the out-of-control battles parents wage over raising children after divorce leave deep and dangerous open wounds and scars on their children long after the parents have moved on, making their children the real casualties of that war. I see these wounds every day in the children who come into my office. Their grades have plummeted. They act out at school and on the ball field. They are angry or sad. Their physicians raise red flags. Their teachers are concerned. I see children, emotionally and behaviorally hurt by the war between their parents, trying frantically to create stability as their world changes too quickly for them to keep up—and so they fall.

There must be a better way.

Making It Work—for the Child

Colin's father, a math whiz who had always been the go-to parent for math and science homework, had an idea. Colin would call Father in California whenever he got stuck with a math problem. Father approached Mother with the idea that he would be the parent primarily responsible for homework. Most school evenings between 7:00 and 8:00, eastern standard time, Colin sat down to do his homework. Father arranged his office schedule to be open between 4:00 and 5:00, Pacific standard time. Father purchased his own set of Colin's textbooks and got Colin a fax machine and scanner so that Colin could send him his worksheets and assignments. Colin and Father spent the first five minutes of homework time reviewing the tasks to be completed that day. Colin would then send his completed work to check. After Dad checked the work, he and Colin would communicate either by phone or online. Periodically, of course, there were problems: Colin would rather play games on the computer than study or, when Father was quizzing him over the phone, he was reading his answers off of a study guide. Father even bought a videocam for Colin's computer so that he could see Colin doing his homework—but somehow Colin never figured out how to make the camera work.

Although Colin now saw his father only a few times a year, the two maintained a consistent, meaningful, real, and ongoing relationship that continued to evolve over time. The consistency of contact about homework taught Colin that both his parents were involved in his life. He saw his parents actively communicate with each other. Yes, they squabbled at times, but they successfully resolved conflicts. Regularity of contact, even through the unconventional technologies of Facebook, faxing, scanning, and cell phones, proved to Colin that his father was involved and caring.

Conversations about homework easily drifted to other topics—sports, friends, extracurriculars. Colin never really understood what it meant for his father to block off work time to help him with his homework, but what he did understand was that the homework hour was his father's way of staying involved in his life. Colin's mother, initially hesitant to give up her role of overseeing his homework, was satisfied with her son's academic progress. Father was exacting about homework performance. Colin would often shout at him over the phone, complaining about being asked to email yet another draft of an English paper. However, that proved the relationship was real; these conflicts could well have materialized had Colin's parents still been together. The conversations between Colin and his father were not forced. There was little of the generic "What did you do in school today?" and "Who did you eat lunch with?" Instead they were focused on Colin's real everyday life. Father talked about his own work and values during their ten-minute breaks from homework. This gave Colin an appreciation of accurate writing and communication skills in the workplace. Colin remembers the day his father forwarded him a poorly written email from a subcontractor bidding on Father's work project, accompanied by Father's explanation of why he had given the bid to another firm.

Now in high school, Colin still has regular contact with his father. Although by now most of Colin's work is independent, Father still edits and reads much of Colin's writing. The 7:00 to 8:00 p.m. time slot is no longer set aside for them; instead Father and Colin schedule other times to review or quiz. Colin knows his father and his father knows him, even though they physically see each other only a handful of times a year. Summer visits now last only a week or two, with Colin joining Father's new family for vacations. Colin's adjustment to school, sports, and social life is good. Colin knows his parents have a respectful, businesslike relationship for discussing significant issues in his life. His mother still worries that Colin may one day get mad at her and announce he wants to move to California. Yet she also knows she will accept this if it is best for her son.

It Should Be All About Love

Colin's positive growth and development are a direct result of two parents creatively and non-conventionally adapting to new situations to insure that their son will have meaningful and caring relationships with both his parents. Their family situation is certainly not perfect and obviously not what either of Colin's parents envisioned life being like when they began their marriage, back in the days of wine and roses. But it's a whole lot better than an unfortunate majority of post-divorce situations. You too can learn a better way of co-parenting.

Raising the Kid You Love with the Ex You Hate draws on my thirty years of experience as a clinical psychologist working with families in transition and conflict to minimize the negative impacts of separation and divorce on their children. This book will teach you the philosophy, the principles, and the methods necessary to raise a healthy child by co-parenting. The goals of co-parenting are simple—to maximize positive outcomes for your child after divorce and to immunize your child as best you can against the ravages of parental hatred.

Raising the Kid You Love with the Ex You Hate demonstrates how you can parent effectively despite the acrimony divorce leaves behind. It helps immunize your children against the ravages of separation and shows warring parents how to develop a new, post-divorce language and healthy style of interaction essential for co-parenting.

Whether you are thinking of separating, are in the process of divorcing, have been divorced for several years, or are trying to develop a parenting plan, this book gives you the tools necessary to raise—together with your ex—the child you both love.

Part One

CO-PARENTING
101

CHAPTER 1

Congratulations, You Are Divorced—Now Start Co-Parenting

If you enjoy fighting with people, you are now in the right position. Probably never before in your life have you been in a place where every decision you make, large or small, is so likely to be challenged by someone else, sometimes for good reasons and sometimes just because this person hates you and doesn't trust a word you say or a thing you do. And to make matters worse, your challenger has a legal agreement that virtually mandates conflict.

Bound by the court, you must not only consult with your ex before doing anything related to your child, but now the two of you must also agree on matters that in the past you likely decided on your own. And the fact is that you and your ex are stuck together, at least until the child reaches maturity and likely for many years after that. Your murderous fantasies are just that—fantasies.

Your ex now is involved in every aspect of your life as a parent: what you feed your kids, how you discipline them, what activities you drive them to, when they see their friends, what time they go to sleep, what kind of clothes they wear, when they visit your family, when they visit your ex's family, how they pray, and when they do their homework.

You now also have new, unanticipated controls on your own life. They affect your earnings and hours at work, how you spend your holidays and vacations, whether or not you can move, your freedom to introduce new people into the life of your family, even whom you have sex with, and when.

After ending your marriage from hell, you don't really want your ex, through a binding custody agreement, controlling your love life. Yet your custody agreement states: "No non-blood family member of the opposite sex shall spend overnight in either parent's residence in the presence of the minor children." That means not only can your new boyfriend not stay over but also that your married sister and her husband have to stay in a hotel when they visit from out of town. You are free to date every other weekend but have to remember that "weekend visitation is subject to out-of-town business plans, in which case seventy-two hours' notice shall be given in writing and visitation shall occur the following weekend."

You may want to get back in shape, so you decide to sign up for an exercise class every other Wednesday night because your ex has visitation every other Wednesday. Of course, that assumes your ex shows up on time, doesn't cancel, and doesn't bring the kids back early. You cannot move without permission: "Both parents agree to remain in the greater metropolitan area with the intent of co-parenting the children."

If you get a raise, you are likely to find yourself back in court to ante up more for child support. If you get fired, you have to prove that this was not a deliberate attempt on your part to increase the support your ex pays.

You now need permission from your ex to take your children to your parents' anniversary party if it falls during your ex's time with the kids. You have to tell the person you hate if you are going to be out of town: "The parties shall inform each other by email seventy-two hours in advance if they are to be away from their permanent residences for greater than a twenty-four-hour time period or if the child is to be away from a residence listed below for greater than a twenty-four-hour time period."

Your custody agreement will make you feel micromanaged. If you want to take a day for yourself, you may have to inform your ex, who, according to your agreement, may have "the right of first refusal": "If I am unable to care for my child for greater than a six-hour time period, other than school or structured activities, and if I enlist the aid of another adult to supervise my child, I agree to inform the other parent seventy-two hours in advance and that parent shall have the first right to care for the child. Should the other parent be unable or refuse to care for the child, such parent shall inform at least twenty-four hours in advance of such."

You really do not want to tell your ex that you are going out of town for the day to meet your new friend's family, but your ex has a legal right to decide whether or not she wants to take the kids that day. So you decide to tell her a week in advance. Then, six days later your ex calls on Friday morning, twenty-four hours before you plan to leave, saying, "Oh no, I can't take the kids tomorrow, but thanks for asking." If a babysitter canceled twenty-four hours in advance without any reason, you would fire her. But now you have a contract that requires you to turn to your ex first before hiring a babysitter when you need one.

Co-Parenting Defined: Why It's for You

You have essentially two realistic choices at this point. You can repeatedly smash your head up against the brick wall of your undesirable situation, or you can compromise and accept a new dynamic that will allow you to preserve a best-case scenario—the concept of co-parenting. In a nutshell, co-parenting is a particular post-divorce arrangement designed to create for the child a sustained relationship with both parents. For the sake of their child, the parents agree to cooperate in order to create a consistent, constructive, and positive atmosphere for their child. Both parents will share, in some manner, in decision making for and physical care of their child.

The co-parenting relationship rests on three broad principles that guide parents after divorce to promote positive growth and development in their children. Challenges to these principles are certainly expected, but adhering to these three guidelines increases the probability of success and positive outcomes for your child.

First, research confirms that children of divorce do better if they maintain positive, meaningful, real, and consistent relationships with both of their parents. But is a fifty-fifty living arrangement better than every other weekend with a midweek visit? Or is an every-other-four-day weekend the best alternative? The answer: There is no credible evidence that any one living arrangement is better for the child than another.

That's because the actual amount of time a child spends with each parent after divorce is not the critical factor determining a child's behavioral and emotional stability. Rather, counting time is a control factor for parents determined to claim days, vacation times, and federal holidays with their child. Fanatically dividing a day down to the minute between two parents may be important to you or to your ex, but it doesn't help your child much. I have yet to see a child, other than one whose parents have drawn her into parental anger and anxious mistrust, who cares whether she spends an extra hour a week with one parent over the other.

Obviously, each parent and child need enough time together to allow a relationship to develop and flourish, but as the story of Colin in the introduction demonstrates, creativity and dedication to the plan you've developed outweigh quantity of time together.

What you as parents consider equal parenting means nothing to your child. What matters in the beginning, the middle, and the end is that each parent develops a relationship with the child, not the quantity of time the parent and child spend together.

Second, there is the principle of reducing discord. The parental relationship has to be as free of conflict as possible, which is hard to do after the contentious battle of the divorce with its fights over child support, visitation, alimony, and custody. Despite all that, you and your ex are still your child's parents, and you must model conflict-free parenting—that is, if you want your child to learn how to solve problems by listening, compromising, and hearing different perspectives in order to effectively reach decisions rather than hanging up the phone, cussing someone out, threatening lawsuits, and ignoring others.

Third, parents must work to assure that both are actively involved in the life of the child and making decisions for the child. The children I see for counseling in my clinical psychology practice are hurt by the divorce, but they are far more damaged by their parents' behaviors that follow. And one of the biggest sources of that pain is the difficulty their parents have in making decisions or in simply being together at important times in the children's lives. These kids worry about which parent to spend their birthday with or which parent to invite to their science fair. Because the parents can't decide, the children feel they have to.

The bottom line is that when adults fight—whether about softball or gymnastics, church or synagogue, organic or non-organic—and when they cannot together effectively set consistent boundaries, rules, and expectations that will allow active and meaningful relationship with both parents, the child suffers.

Rule 1: Your Child Needs Both Parents

Michael was a fourth-grader when his parent's contentious divorce began. Father, a powerful executive diagnosed with bipolar disorder, had a number of affairs and relationships throughout the marriage, many of which Mother knew about but excused in exchange for a life of financial comfort and security. When Michael was seven, Father had another child with one of the two other women he was having active relationships with at that time. His trips out of town for business became more frequent in the last two years of the marriage. One Thanksgiving, when he told his wife he needed to work over the weekend, Mother offered to take the children to his office so he could spend time with his family. Father refused, saying he was forced to work and detailing the number of meetings he had scheduled over the holiday weekend. Mother wised up, hired a private investigator, and discovered Father living with another woman on his weekends at the office. She then filed for divorce.

The bitter divorce battle that followed was over money, not custody. After weeks of confrontation and denials, Michael's father admitted he was having an affair but neglected to say that he was living with another woman and that they already had a two-year-old. Michael soon learned of Father's double life and that he had a stepbrother. An A/B student in third and fourth grades, Michael's grades quickly plummeted to B's and C's. For the first time, Michael began to get in trouble in school. He continued to play soccer and baseball but without his old enthusiasm and success.

Mother argued that given Father's immoral and illegal relationship with the girlfriend and the baby, Michael should have no contact with his father. The courts decided otherwise, giving Father every-other-weekend visitations, provided Father not be with an unmarried, non-related woman overnight in Michael's presence. Father was also given the right to daily phone contact with Michael. Of course, from the third visitation on, Father broke the court order. Father's girlfriend came to "visit" and would stay over to care for his son. Mother filed contempt of court charges against Father. That began a regular pattern of court battles and attorney agreements, brokered and continually broken, until the financial settlement was arranged and the parents divorced. Father married his girlfriend the weekend following his divorce, and Michael was now legally allowed to stay in the house with his "new" stepmother and stepbrother.

Michael's parents' post-separation relationship was never a pleasant one. Mother felt cheated on during her marriage and in the divorce settlement. Her dreams of financial stability were shattered. Unfortunately she showed much of her bitterness and anger to Michael. Mother's selling the family Suburban and million-dollar home and going back to work were "all your father's fault." Father's phone calls to Michael were awkward and irregular. Mother screened calls; often the phone was not answered. Father, long removed from much of Michael's life, didn't have much to say when he finally reached Michael on the phone. After the typical "What did you do in school today?" and "How was soccer practice?" their conversations faltered and failed. Father got angry about Michael's sliding grades and athletic performance and blamed Mother. Mother flared back in anger, blaming Father for all of his past sins. Michael, aware that his parents would argue over his phone calls with Father, began to say he didn't want to talk to his father anymore. The parents continued to blame each other. Soon Mother was back in court requesting an end to phone time and a shortening of the weekend visitations due to "Michael's level of emotional distress." The court, frustrated by the parents' bickering, ordered a psychological evaluation of Michael's needs.

Michael, bright and articulate, was pretty up front about his needs. Even while blaming his father for his parents' divorce, he still liked visiting his stepbrother and really wanted a stronger relationship with his father. But he worried that if he talked to his father regularly on the phone and showed how happy he was to see him, his mother would be upset. He knew he hurt his father when he said they had nothing to talk about on the phone, but Michael felt saying that made his mother happier. The court ordered Michael to maintain contact. Counseling with the mother helped her see how her anger toward her ex was hurting Michael.

Although tension remained between the parents, Michael eventually developed a regular, ongoing, substantial relationship with his father. The parents continued to fight over money, but Michael, now age thirteen, seems more self-assured and confident.

The child's perception of an ongoing and meaningful relationship with both parents is the most significant factor in raising a healthy child after divorce. With the exception of some horrific abusive relationships—and I will argue later that, even after some abusive relationships, it is still important for the child to develop and maintain a relationship with both parents—a child's knowledge of both her parents counts more for her healthy adjustment and sound mental health than anything else that I have seen in more than thirty years of practice. Your arguments that your ex is dysfunctional, angry, neglectful, always late; that he feeds the child only hot dogs, ignores the kid to be with his girlfriend, has done nothing to deserve the contact; that she is depressed, picks fights—none of these factors outweigh the strong developmental need of the child to be emotionally connected to both parents. You may hate your ex's guts for the horrible qualities you now see in her, but the positive qualities you loved when you first met and married are now characteristics of your child's own personality and temperament and need to be fostered. It doesn't really matter what you think of your former spouse. If you want your child to grow healthy emotionally, succeed academically, and develop socially, your child needs to maintain an emotional bond and connection with your ex.

And don't try to teach your ex how to maintain that bond, either. If you couldn't do it while you were married, you are certainly not going to be able to do it now that you are divorced. You are not going to change the quality of the relationship between your ex and your child. You are not going to get him to check homework rather than just ask if it is done. You are not going to get him to notice that the TV is on all the time. You will not get him to stop taking your son to inappropriate movies. This is your ex's relationship with the child, and you can't change it. If your ex is ever going to learn that R-rated movies are not great for ten-year-olds, he will learn it from someone else, not from you. In case you haven't noticed, he doesn't pay much attention to what you say. I have seen so many divorced parents frustrated: No matter what they tell their ex, the ex doesn't listen. The parenting books and articles they send over get returned unopened and unread. Of course, there must be forums for the two parents to discuss critical issues in the life of the child, but one ex cannot overtly or covertly keep the child away from the other because of the bitterness of the divorce or because Mom doesn't do things the way Dad thinks they must be done.

Remember: it is not *your* perception of their relationship that matters, anyway. You may think that because your ex is always late and seems to plop your child in front of the television on visitations that your daughter has no relationship with him, but in fact she does. This relationship may not be ideal, and it may not be the kind of relationship you think you have with your daughter or the kind of relationship you want your ex to have with her, but it is a relationship, and your daughter will see it as such. That a relationship exists far outweighs the perceived quality of the relationship in determining the emotional and psychological outcomes of divorce for your children.

And besides, your perception of your former spouse probably doesn't match your child's, unless you pressure him to adopt it. To you, your ex is irresponsible, immature, inconsiderate, and emotionally abusive, the guy who had affairs during your marriage and who hasn't paid child support for months, who cancels his scheduled visits with your child, and who has yet to show up for a parent-teacher conference. But to your child he is "daddy." Living out your anger toward your ex through your child—even when justified and verified by four court hearings in three different states because he is always late for visitation and is not paying child support—may give you your sweet revenge, but it ends up hurting your child.

Instead you might have to act a little schizophrenic at times to pull off the delicate act of hating your ex while supporting her relationship with your child. But remember: you support this relationship not because your ex deserves it, but because your child needs it to immunize him from the potentially emotional, behavioral, and social ravages so many children experience after divorce.

The development of a meaningful parent/child relationship—as perceived by the child—is what is important, even if it's not that important to the parent. Your ex may have remarried, had three more children, and stopped paying child support a long time ago. Your ex may behave as if he doesn't care, but it is your child's perception of a relationship with that parent that is important. It would be great if you liked the kind of relationship they have, but the fact that you don't is probably one of the reasons you are divorced.

Your child needs to develop her own relationship with and opinion of your ex, her parent. You can't force this relationship, and your trying to shape it creates a level of tension that disrupts the life of your child.

You don't have to like your ex, but if you are going to co-parent successfully, you will have to deal with her.

Rule 2: Reduce Parental Conflict After the Separation

Since their parents divorced, Chris, fourteen, and Addison, sixteen, had been raised in a virtual war zone. The children had limited memories of parental conflict pre-divorce, other than heated arguments when Mother found out about an affair Father had. But after the divorce, conflict was all they knew.

First, their mother reverted to her maiden name, and then she asked her children if they also wanted to change their names, a move the court blocked. She called their father "him" and "Mr. Smith." Mother left the children messages saying, "Mr. Smith called to say that you left your jacket at the house he shares with the whore."

Although the parents had joint legal custody which mandated that together they were to discuss, review, and implement decisions about their children, the parents communicated only through lawyers and when in court. Each parent insisted that the children take sides. When Addison sided with her mother, "Mr. Smith" quickly abandoned Addison and put all his energy toward connecting with Chris.

Mother referred to the time her son and daughter spent with her ex as "court-ordered visitation time with Mr. Smith," and "Mr. Smith" stretched reality, calling the time he did not have his children "visitation at your old house." The exes shared driving duties, but neither parent allowed the other near his/her primary residence. Instead, one parent always dropped the children off at the corner of the street of the ex's home. From there the children marched, suitcases in hand, up to the house of their other parent, their home for part of each week.

For the first three years each parent actually videotaped all transitions. The children would have to remain in their father's car with the radio on an all-talk radio station (just what kids love to listen to in a car) until the video camera would record it giving the time. The children had to be returned to the mother's on Sundays by 6:00 p.m. So Father would make them sit in the car until the traffic and weather report came on at 5:58 p.m. He then hustled them out the door, and they dashed home, ringing the doorbell at 6:00 p.m., not a second before or after.

When she turned sixteen, Addison announced she was no longer going on visitations with her dad, because she knew the courts were hesitant to enforce visitations after age sixteen. Chris then deteriorated emotionally. He hid in his father's closets and called his mother secretly. His mother taught Chris code words he could use to report on "Mr. Smith's" behavior, all related to how Chris felt physically. If the girlfriend was visiting the house over the weekend, Chris would say he had a headache. If father was yelling or being mean, Chris had a stomachache. If the father was physically disciplining Chris or not letting him do what he wanted to—the mother conflated these as abuses—Chris would report he had a fever. Prior to each visit, Mother would test Chris on the codes and how he had to report on his "health" over the weekend.

It was no big surprise that shortly after Addison stopped going to see their father, Chris began getting sick before his visits. He no longer waited to use code words while with his father; instead, in advance he said he had a stomachache, a headache, or a fever. After two missed visitations Mr. Smith filed a contempt-of-court charge, accusing his ex of withholding Chris from visitations.

The court ordered that Chris had to go on his scheduled visitations. And at first Chris stayed the entire day with his father, especially after Dad bought tickets to college basketball games for Chris and a friend. But as bedtime approached, Chris called his mother, complained that he was ill, and asked to go home. Within four visits, Chris was down to only having lunch with his father before getting "sick" and returning to his mother's house. When Dad suggested that Chris was only feigning illness—after all, he had a nearly perfect school attendance record—Chris started getting sick at school as well and would miss school the Thursday or Friday of the week he was to see his father.

Within four months Chris was doing virtual drive-by visits. His father, hoping for any type of connection, agreed to Chris visiting for just a few hours on Saturday afternoons. But soon Chris was calling on Saturday mornings to say he did not feel well. When Mr. Smith insisted Chris come over anyway, Mom would drive Chris, still wearing the sweatpants that he slept in and clutching a box of tissues, to Mr. Smith's. Chris would get out of the car and run up the street to the apartment complex while his mother videotaped him. Chris would ring the doorbell, tell his father he was ill, turn around, and jog back to Mom's car.

After Father protested in court, Chris agreed to visit, but usually entered the apartment, turned on the TV to watch one movie, and refused to eat or to communicate with his father. Mr. Smith could not stop himself from openly damning and blaming his ex's parenting style for Chris's behaviors.

The weekend after Chris finished eighth grade, he invented a new scheme. He now faithfully jogged up to his father's apartment and taped a note to the door indicating he had shown up for his court-ordered visit but was not staying because he was ill. Mr. Smith would be waiting at the door, begging or threatening Chris to enter, but to no avail. Chris jogged back to his mother's car, engine still running, and returned to their home.

As Chris's story makes clear, the level of post-divorce parental conflict impacts the child's emotional and behavioral stability. Despite no longer seeing his father, Chris continued to miss school. He could not manage the stresses of high school, and frequently he went home sick. His grades dropped from A's and B's to C's. Chris became anxious about remaining alone in a room and would no longer sleep over at friends' houses. He ended up internalizing the pattern of conflicts and the tensions he learned from his parents' post-divorce relationship. In the end, conflict, anger, and avoidance became not just the way Chris dealt with his father, but the way he dealt with the world around him.

Surely, no parent would ever wish this for a child, and I know that's not what either of Chris's parents wanted for either of their children. But they simply were unable to acknowledge that their animosity toward each other was hurting their children.

The hard, cold truth is that the level of post-divorce parental conflict and strife dramatically impacts the behaviors and emotions of the child. Children who experience parental conflict after separation or divorce do much worse than children who see their divorced parents in a businesslike, appropriate relationship with each other.

In order to achieve the latter, parents should approach their relationship as two equal business partners concerned about a product, their child. There is no room for emotions in this type of relationship. Both partners want their product to succeed. So they set aside their hostilities from prior failed partnerships and overlook personality and stylistic differences, which can only hinder and not guarantee the successful launch of their product—the child.

Surprisingly, parental conflict before divorce, within limits, does not appear to be as predictive of the child's future outcome. The exception is if there has been child abuse or extreme neglect prior to the divorce, which will have a significant impact on the child's future development. But if the child grows up seeing conflict and arguments between the parents while they were married, the child comes to understand why the parents divorced. It is as if the child says, "I got it. Mom and Dad argued all the time. That's why they split up." But constant bickering after separation and divorce, when the only remaining binding connection between the parents is the child, has a significant impact on the child's welfare. After all, were there no child from this marriage, the exes would have no need to have a relationship post-divorce—and at some point, the child comes to recognize this.

From the child's perspective, once the divorce is settled and done, there is really only one thing to argue about: the child. The divorce decree settles all financial issues, and by the time it is sealed, blame for the breakup has also most likely been determined. If the parents are supposedly moving on with their lives but they continue to fight, the child will blame himself for the parental conflict. While blaming your ex for your child's problems may help you feel better, the anger perpetuates your child's self-blame and, unfortunately, helps create behavioral and emotional difficulties.

Children perceive anger between parents in several ways. It begins with names. Do not refer to your ex as a son-of-a-bitch, bastard, Mr. Smith, Ms. Smith, that whore, or "your father" with a sneer in your voice. You once loved this person, and you produced children together. Show respect for your ex's role as your child's parent. It is respectable and responsible to speak of your ex to your child by the name you used before the divorce: "Mom called to say there is a lot of traffic" or "Dad says he will be about fifteen minutes late." These are appropriate remarks to your child. But telling your daughter "Once again your selfish father has the nerve to show he doesn't even care enough about you or me to get here on time" is not.

Your ex's selfish and narcissistic behaviors do not create the problems your son or daughter will develop. Rather, the problems are created by your failure to let go and move beyond your perceptions and characterizations of your ex as selfish and narcissistic.

Your child, in fact, needs to see a functional parental relationship despite your divorce. You deal with selfish narcissists at work every day without showing excessive anger. Do so now with your ex for the sake of your child.

Rule 3: Both Parents Make Decisions

I think Marc, a ten-year-old I saw in outpatient treatment because of his acting-out behaviors following parental separation, said it the best. While his mom was scheduling a follow-up therapy appointment on a Friday morning, he piped in: "It can't be on Fridays, Mom; that's motions day." Marc was referring to the day in many court systems where very brief, single-point arguments are brought before a judge for resolution. The parents had been in conflict and in court so often for motions days that Marc thought every Friday some judge he never saw or met made decisions about his life. He had come to believe that his parents were powerless. Sadly, he thought only the lawyers and judges made decisions about his life and well-being.

The child who thinks his parents can only make decisions when "my lawyer says so" will likely have a bad outcome. Co-parents must make decisions together about the child they love, and they must refuse to transfer their responsibility to the courts, lawyers, psychologists, and social workers. Making decisions about the kid you love with the ex you hate forces you as parents to discuss issues, to compromise, and to reach consensus so that, in the end, your child will know that together his mom and his dad decided how he should be raised.

That's why the third and final major factor influencing the child's likelihood of having a healthier outcome post-divorce is the child's perception that both parents are jointly involved in decision making. This does not mean that all parenting decisions have to be made together. The primary physical custodial parent should usually decide whether a certain dress is appropriate and whether his daughter needs a haircut.

1: CONGRATULATIONS, YOU ARE DIVORCED—NOW START CO-PARENTING

However, the child needs to know that when it comes to major issues in her life, the two parents make the decisions together.

With co-parenting, the details of the child's life work out in much the same fashion as those of children in married, intact families. After the infant's first haircut or two, usually only one parent takes responsibility for getting the child haircuts. Only one parent takes charge of school-supply shopping. But after divorce, both parents have to make certain that their households have the supplies needed for schoolwork: the papers, pencils, glue, and markers. Both parents need children's clothing in their homes, but they need to communicate about what each has purchased. Most likely the child needs only one winter coat, but he does need jeans and tee shirts in both of his homes.

While one co-parent may not like the style or label the other buys, in the end the clothes belong to the child and each co-parent ends up losing some control. If Mom buys her daughter Lucky brand jeans and Dad buys his at Wal-Mart, the Lucky jeans are sure to spend some time at Dad's house. It is fine to discuss clothing preferences with your ex, but be prepared: you probably won't get far in these discussions. Mom may argue that the child looks better and has greater social status in designer jeans, that Dad is too cheap to splurge for them, and that he is harming the child by not buying them. Dad will counter that Mom is shallow and a spendthrift, and that soon the child will outgrow the jeans and need new ones, anyway.

Know that this argument is not going to get resolved. It is far better to swallow the frustration and periodically redistribute the child's clothing between the two households without involving the child. Parents could also agree to create a joint clothing fund and compromise on the brand names. What is most essential is not to denigrate your ex's choices of clothing in front of your child. What is far worse to the child than wearing Wal-Mart and Lucky jeans on different days is hearing his parents fail to make a decision about something as relatively inconsequential as his clothing.

What decisions should co-parents make jointly? Court orders that list the areas of co-parenting decision making often include such major areas of the child's life as education, health, extracurricular activities, religious training, summer activities, and moral issues. These areas of the child's life are sufficiently and perhaps deliberately vague so that many co-parents end up in conflict over the details of what is included and excluded from this list. Are braces required for the child's health or are they cosmetic? If they are necessary for health, then the co-parents have to agree that they are needed and jointly choose the orthodontist. But if they are needed only for cosmetic purposes, then one parent can decide without consulting the other. Is a reading tutor, not required by the school, an educational decision or a parental option? Does taking the child to a specific church only when she is with one parent fall under religious training, or is it a family activity with that parent? Most co-parents would likely concede that they have to agree on their daughter's sleep-away camp, since sleeping at camp would affect both parents' time with their child. However, if she spends two weeks at Dad's during the summer, can he send her to Bible camp for a week or even to a scouts' sleep-away camp during his time without consulting with Mom? Co-parenting demands that the child perceive both parents as actively involved in making these decisions. The child's understanding—that both his parents work together to make decisions about his welfare—can occur only when both parents are actively involved in the child's life in a consistent and meaningful manner and when the parental relationship, as distinct from the exes' relationship with the former spouse and lover, has limited conflict.

Effective post-divorce communication patterns help the child see that both parents are actively, jointly involved in making decisions about his life. When there are conflicts, Dad has to tell his daughter, "I need to discuss this issue with your mom." Mom says: "I have to talk to Dad about your behavior, and we will decide what to do." Hearing this message from both parents teaches the child that his parents remain in discussion about his life and make decisions about him jointly. Schedule five minutes each week to talk to your ex about child-related issues, including the small details of his schedule for the coming week. Do this every week, no matter what else is going on in your lives. Discuss only scheduling and the immediate needs of the child—that he needs extra help with his math homework because he got a C, that he has had a cough and when he should take his cough medicine. This is not the time to discuss the co-parents' conflicts over child support payments. Make certain the child sees her parents working together on these decisions. Outcomes are much worse when children perceive or believe that it is "others" who make decisions about their lives.

After divorce your child needs a relationship with both parents. He needs to see you and your ex parenting without conflict and together making important decisions in his life.

CHAPTER 2

What Your Child Needs to Know — and What He Doesn't

Ron, a forty-seven-year-old former Wall Street broker, sauntered into my office, no longer looking like he belonged on Wall Street. With tattered jeans, earrings, and tattoos, he explained that Zoey, his twelve-year-old daughter was refusing to have much contact with him since he moved out of the house. A four-page letter Zoey wrote to her father explained that she would see him only for short time periods and never ever in a restaurant or anywhere in public they could be seen together.

When I asked Ron what he told Zoey about the divorce, he replied, "The truth": that her trusted therapist of the past two years was probably having a lesbian affair with her mother. He then threw in for good measure that her mother was an "alcoholic, castrating bitch who drank herself to sleep every night after Zoey went to bed."

His angry disclosure sent Zoey into shock; she shut down completely. For three days Zoey feigned illness and could not go to school. She absolutely refused to see her father. A flurry of phone calls from Ron forced Zoey to power down her cell phone. She reluctantly agreed to speak to her father when he showed up at the door of her mother's apartment the night before they were scheduled to have a joint parent-child meeting in my office.

Ron apologized to Zoey for hurting her but swore that he had told the truth. He then added, "I hate your mother. She's a bitch. I hope she dies. There is a special place in hell for her." Not surprisingly, Zoey ran to her bedroom sobbing, locked the door, and refused to see or talk to her father.

Your child's perspective about how well your co-parenting arrangement will work begins at the beginning—with the extremely difficult task of telling your child about the impending divorce and separation. How you indicate to the child the significant and radical changes about to occur sets the tone for the co-parenting experiment.

You need to be honest, real, and effective as you convey the news that the two of you plan to separate and divorce. Many parents think it best to break the news gradually. They begin by telling their child that they are merely separating. If you are not yet committed to divorce, then that is the fair thing to say. But if divorce is indeed imminent and you and your spouse know that reconciliation is no longer possible, then be honest with your child even though this may create a higher level of anxiety and worry for your child at first. Tell him that while Mommy and Daddy love their little boy, their marriage to each other must end.

Honesty is so important at this point because divorce breaks a primary trust. Children instinctively believe that "no matter what, my parents will always be there to support and protect me." Divorce shatters this fundamental trust that underlies the child's universe. With this news, the child's world is irrevocably altered. The quake of divorce reverberates throughout the early stages of parental divorce and separation. Questions and disturbing thoughts now rush through the child's mind: "They always said they would be here for me . . . . What else have my parents lied to me about? I thought they would always be together, that this is my home, this is my family. Now, with one sentence—'Mom and I are getting a divorce'—the world I knew has broken apart. They say they will continue to love me, but they used to say they loved each other. If they can stop loving each other, will they stop loving me? They said we would always be together; now we will be separate. They said I will always be with them, but can parents also divorce their kid?"

Once your child realizes trust can be broken, she immediately begins to look for other situations to doubt, or to suspect you of breaking her trust. "What else will you tell me now that is also not true?" Your child's mind begins to race, seeking out nuances, questioning other things you have said and have promised. The child is assailed by doubts. Have you told her other untruths? Have you broken other primary trusts?

That's why you and your soon-to-be ex need to sit down together to tell your child you plan to separate and divorce, and your ability to convey this news together in a caring and relatively non-hostile manner sets the tone for the child's perception of the future co-parenting decisions you and your ex will make together. How effectively you and your ex deal with your child at this moment may well predict the effectiveness of your future co-parenting decisions.

Given the tension within the marriage, one parent will often plead: "I can't possibly be in the room with my ex and keep it together to talk to my child." But the child needs to hear and to see that this is a process the entire family undertakes together. Your message should be not only that we agreed on this separation and divorce, but also that we love and care for you, our child, and that together we have made decisions that are best for you and that will determine your future.

How Much to Say

There are many things not to say to your child at this time. Mom, don't make disparaging remarks about Dad. Dad, don't explain to your son all Mom's flaws and faults. This is not a time to tell your child that you will be penniless, that you have to go back to work, that his dad is a lying, cheating alcoholic, or that your in-laws, your child's grandparents, never loved him anyway. Your child does need to know the details of the radical changes he is about to experience, but that does not mean that you should expect or demand that your child support you in your hurt and your anger at your ex.

You do not need to tell your child what you think of your ex. Oh, you think your intentions are good. Your child needs this information: "She needs to know what she is up against, to protect herself." But when you belittle your ex before your child, you damage your child. You may not see the similarities between your child and your ex, but your child does. If you take up a verbal hatchet to destroy your ex, you have destroyed your child.

Do not blame your about-to-be ex. Even if your ex has been having an affair with her boss for the last three years and you have just gotten hold of her phone records to prove it, or if you have just discovered credit card bills from sex toy shops, do not share this with your child. One of the first rules of becoming co-parents is not ever to say to your child that you blame your ex for the divorce. Often, one parent will say: "But I don't want the divorce. I didn't agree to this and it is all his fault. If I am supposed to be honest with my child and what I tell my child must be truthful, how do I tell my child about the divorce? Shouldn't I say it is because of her affair? His alcoholism? Her anger management problems?"

The answer is no. First, it is only your perception that the affair, alcoholism, and anger management are the reasons for the divorce. Your spouse surely has a very different list of causes for the divorce. Conveying two different messages to your child about why his parents are divorcing burdens the child and is irrelevant to him anyway. What is relevant is how his life is about to change. Your discussions must focus on future living arrangements and plans, not on the past. What you say to your child about the divorce or about your ex has to be the truth, but it need not be the whole truth. The entire truth—the lies, the affairs, the emotional battles—is the basis for an adult war. Don't send your child into this battle. Save her from this emotional violence.

Your child needs to know only one truth: "Mom and Dad don't love each other anymore, the way that moms and dads need to love each other to stay together." Your child has absolutely no need to know the reasons Mom and Dad don't love each other. When is it time to share? When your child comes home from college and asks, "What really did happen between you and Mom?" Then, if you still want to, you may convey your perceptions to her about your marriage to her mother. Until then, the simple truth, unembellished by your perspective, is far more helpful to your child than a blow-by-blow replay of "he said, she said," aimed at forcing your child to choose between her parents or to play the role of judge.

When and How to Tell Them

There is never a good time to break the news. There is always some significant event coming round the bend—an upcoming birthday, holiday, vacation, school test, parental trip, important soccer match, grandparent visit, best friend's birthday party, or anniversary of a family death.

Several days before one of the parents moves out of the primary residence is the time to break the news. That marks the beginning of the transition to co-parenting. After telling the child, the parents should not physically remain together. Parents may stay in the same household for several days, but they should sleep in separate bedrooms. This signals the coming changes to the child. The changes should happen within the next few days. And even if your child is a strapping adolescent who lifts weights and is on the football team, he should not help you move out. In fact, it is best if the move occurs when the child is not at home.

If the stresses of the marriage have been obvious, the child will get it. An adolescent may well react with some understanding and compassion, and attempt to ally with her parents to offer emotional support. A younger child may only be confused and disoriented. Your job is not to win your child as an ally but to convey information and support the child in his own time of distress.

What should be paramount in this moment, as you tell your child that you plan to separate and divorce, is your capacity to comfort your child, to show him that, while the rules have changed, new guidelines and new structures are already being set up to regulate his life from now on. Be concrete and factual. Tell your child that you are divorcing and explain how this will affect her daily and weekly routine. Give her the information she needs to help her ground this new and scary reality. Throughout the divorce process, your child needs to see both parents making decisions about his life. This must start with this most difficult moment—when both parents sit together with the child, even in the midst of their great stress, hostility, and turmoil, and together tell their child that they are separating and then outline the family's new living arrangements.

But there are important rules to follow in timing this conversation. Do not have this conversation at bedtime—unless you want your child to be up all night, emotional and reactive. You need to pick a time when not only are both parents there to convey the news but also when you can return together at least once and preferably twice or more later that day, in conversations that are an hour or two apart, to answer questions, to reassure your child that this is not her fault, and to explain again what you envision for the future. Over the weekend in the early afternoon is often a very good time to tell the child.

What She Thinks When You Say "Divorce"

What does the child hear when she and her parents sit down to have perhaps the most painful conversation the family has ever experienced? Often it is akin to listening to an orchestra warming up. At first, the child hears a cacophony of loud and confusing sounds. The information these sounds convey is so overwhelming to the child that she will manage only to grasp certain pieces at first. But, as with an orchestra's rehearsal, after the various musicians have finished warming up, the sounds come together and a piece of recognizable music is played. So too, for the child, the discrete pieces of information her parents have just conveyed come together into some kind of understandable whole.

It is especially critical in this initial discussion, as well as in all future conversations, to do everything possible to prevent your child from blaming himself for the divorce. Children believe that the world revolves around them, that they bear responsibility for the events—both positive and negative—that have occurred in their lives. Children can all too easily come to believe, almost magically, that they caused their parents' separation and divorce.

Campbell, seven years old, was sitting on my office couch, trying to learn how to get along better with children on the playground. In the midst of describing how difficult it was to remember which parent was supposed to help her with her homework that night, she whispered: "Can I tell you a secret that really bothers me?" She knew why her parents had divorced. Last year, her two-year-old brother was really annoying her during dinner, so she pushed him, and he spilled his milk all over the floor. Campbell vividly remembered her parents' argument over who would clean it up. Her mom had screamed: "You never do anything around here. You are never home." Her dad had yelled back: "If you did a better job with the kids, they wouldn't be fighting all the time." Several months later her parents announced their separation. Campbell knew why: it was her fault—she had hit her brother, he had spilled his milk, and that had caused the fight and then the divorce.

Campbell blamed herself; she had made her parents yell at each other. In her mind, that one argument had caused the divorce. She had so internalized these emotions and carried them within her throughout the separation process that she needed weeks of hearing repeatedly from both her parents that the divorce was not her fault. Only then did she begin to relax around her classmates on the playground.

In this very first conversation about separation and divorce with your child, lay out a broad outline of future plans to co-parent. Mom and Dad together tell their child that from now on he will live separately with each of them. Together you explain what this means. This is *not* the time to overwhelm your child with specifics—that he spends every other weekend with Dad; that weekends begin on Thursday at 6:00 p.m., that Mom takes charge of Boy Scouts and religious school. Your child will already be utterly overwhelmed by the news. She cannot possibly effectively understand anything more than "We are your parents. We love you. Although we will be living separately, you are now and always will be a part of both of our lives. You will live some of the time with Mom and some of the time with Dad. You will continue to go to your same school. We will both take you to your friends' houses, and your friends will come over to both of our houses to hang out. You will still play on the same softball team. We will both show up for games and practices as we have in the past. The main change is that we will be living separately, and you will be spending time with each of us in our homes."

2: WHAT YOUR CHILD NEEDS TO KNOW—AND WHAT HE DOESN'T

Showing emotion is perfectly appropriate in this conversation. If you cry, you give your child permission to cry too. Of course, emotionality should not block the message that must be conveyed.

Expect your child to be shocked and confused. After this initial discussion, your child needs time to process. If you have more than one child, your children may bond together. They may want to find a comfortable space to console each other and to take stock as they deal with their confusion and wonder what will happen next. Give your child space; understand the child's need to react. You and your ex have had months to think about the separation and divorce, but your child is just learning about it now and needs time to grapple with the news.

The second sit-down with the child should take place an hour or two after the first. Your child will likely ask why the separation and divorce is occurring. The temptation is to blame others, maybe to indicate this is not what you want. Again, tell the truth but not the whole truth. Be general with the reasons but deal concretely with the new situation. Explain that relationships are difficult and complex and that separation rarely occurs for a single reason. When a marriage is unhappy, moms and dads need to be apart. Then sketch out the child's new living arrangements. Mom has a condo nearby. Explain that the child will live there on weekends and some school days. Reassure your daughter—she will still play on the same soccer team and go to the same school. Promise your son that he will still see his same friends. Remember: Children are innately narcissistic. The world revolves around them.

Still do not give every detail of the separation agreement; the child has no need to know right now that at 1:00 p.m. on Christmas every other year he will transition from one parent to the other. Repeat to your child that both of you love him and that he will see both of you on Christmas.

Your First Steps as a Co-Parent

Over the next day or two, each parent needs time alone with the child. Each must reassure the child that the divorce is not the child's fault. Remember again that it is very important not to blame or disparage the other parent in these conversations.

Continue to be honest and reassuring about what you know and also about what you do not know yet. If you know the house will be sold, tell your child. But don't talk about what high school your sixth-grader will attend. Now is not the time to discuss alternating yearly Easter breaks between the parents. What your child needs are specific details about the short term, the coming weeks. Expect that each conversation will allow for more information and for your child's greater comprehension.

Deal concretely with the next steps: detailing where and when and with whom your child will live. He needs to know that he will still play on his baseball team, which parent will get him to his friends' house on Saturday night, and how his world will operate in the wake of this upheaval. You will need to give the child a calendar for the next several weeks. It should not have specific times and places, but rather the conceptual framework for his future living arrangements. It should show that one week he lives with Mom, the next with Dad, or that she will be staying here in her house during the week, but that on many weekends she will be staying with Dad in his new apartment. Explain that this is a permanent, not a temporary, arrangement. Understand that your child imagines that this nightmarish situation will end soon, that she fantasizes already that the separation will be only temporary, and that no way will her parents permanently divorce. But if the parents have decided that the marriage will end, then you must tell this to the child now and make clear that these new living arrangements are permanent and real.

2: WHAT YOUR CHILD NEEDS TO KNOW—AND WHAT HE DOESN'T

To create two households for the child, the parents need to share some of the child's personal belongings and effects. For example, if there are two sets of sheets for the child's bed, then one set goes to the new household. Leave some Barbies in each home. Take some Legos to the new place. Some toys, some favorite cups, some child's dishes should be divided between the two households. The intent is not to replicate the child's old home in his new physical environment. Over time, the child's second home will acquire its own identity. But for now the goal is to make the child as comfortable as possible. Having her sleep on her usual sheets in both homes helps achieve that. Your new home needs a bed, clothing, and personal effects. While you do not want to strip the primary residence, do take some things of significance to your child to the new home.

Don't take the child to see your new place immediately, but introduce him to it gradually. Describe it to your child and drive by. Next time drive around the neighborhood. If it is close to your old home, point that out. If not, highlight the places your son will like—a new playground, the condo's swimming pool. Make a brief stop at the new apartment. The next time your daughter can stay for lunch and spend the afternoon. After that, she will sleep over in her new bed with her old sheets.

Know that your child will not want to live in the new place. The conflict for your child is how to be comfortable in her new environment, yet be secure with both parents. Both parents have to encourage and support the child's living in both households. When the child complains, "I don't really like Daddy's new apartment," Mom must not agree, "You're right, it's terrible." Instead, Mom's job is to answer that both parents care about and love the child and to emphasize that both parents have decided it is best for the child to live in both households.

What will the child need in each of her homes? Obviously items like clothing, cosmetics, entertainment, comfort toys, and games. We all know it takes some time to set up a new apartment. For a few weeks a child can sleep at her dad's in a sleeping bag or on an air mattress, just like when she has sleepovers at her friends' homes. But that air mattress must give way to a new bed for the child as soon as possible. Then take her shopping to buy things for her new room. Even if the apartment is fairly barren, even if you think, "I will only live in this apartment for a little while, so I don't want to waste money fixing it up," you must make your child's second home as comfortable as you can. Your short-term rental is your child's reality. He needs to feel it offers him the sense of security of coming home.

Often the question of introducing roommates pops up. Dad moved out and rented a room in a group home with people he barely knows. By no means should he bring these acquaintances into the child's life at first. Your son is already dealing with the turmoil of disruption; adding these strangers to that mix just increases his sense of the commotion going on in his life. By the same token, this is also not the time to take your child to your girlfriend's house or to leave him watching TV while you go out on a date.

If you want to co-parent effectively, it is imperative that you create a comfortable, safe, and secure environment where your child will continue, when he lives with you, the developmental trajectory of childhood. You are the one who is separating and divorcing, not your child. If you cannot manage to create that comfortable environment for your child in your new home, then you should co-parent without sleepovers until you can set it up.

Divorcing parents do not always realize that their living arrangements will transition over time, that the first week of separation need not start the new living arrangements.

Above all else, do not insist on having your child sleep in your new digs just to pull your child away from your ex. Co-parenting means meaningful contact with your child, joint decision making, and continually demonstrating to the child that both her parents care for and are concerned about her.

Put the child's needs above your own, understand his developmental issues, and make decisions appropriate for your child.

CHAPTER 3

Money Matters: Child Support Is for the Child

After what appeared to be a relatively stress-free divorce, Christina and Ross decided that co-parenting would be the best for their two young children. With Ross building a successful radiology practice and his schedule rotating, they agreed the children would visit him on his days off and that weekend visitations would be set at the beginning of each month when Ross got his on-call schedule. Christina, a nurse, had limited her practice to part-time work over the past several years in order to stay at home to raise the children.

Everything was going fine until Ross's parents began to fear losing their only grandchildren. Ross's father, a very successful surgeon, pushed his son to seek greater control over the children by offering to hire a full-time nanny. Ross's mother also offered to help watch the children during the day. Ross's father then spent huge amounts of money on attorney fees to try to win grandparent visitation rights. When that failed, he tried to get sole custody of the children given to Ross.

When Christina's Christian parents, equally determined and angry, began to take the children to church, Ross's Jewish father tried even more forcefully to claim authority over his grandchildren. With the grandparents at war, the co-parenting Ross and Christina had first planned fell by the wayside. When Ross had to work an extra weekend shift, his parents claimed his visitation rights. Christina refused.

Ross's parents, who had funded his end of the divorce proceedings and legal battles, now stopped paying child support to Christina, opting instead to place funds into a closed trust for their grandchildren.

Multiple contempt hearings and dueling accusations later, a settlement emerged—similar to Ross's and Christina's original divorce plan—at a cost of an additional $150,000 in legal and expert-testimony fees. When Ross's parents, who still funded him, refused to pay Christina's child support, the court had to step in and garnish Ross's salary.

The acrimony quickly and dramatically distorted the relationship between Ross and Christina, which, of course, adversely affected the children. Previously they had seen their parents chatting when they moved from one household to another. Now the parents refused to even acknowledge each other. Ross's usual phone calls from the hospital announcing that he was running late had been met with benign comments in the past. Now Christina launched into a tirade about Ross's lack of responsibility and care for his children. What had been a harmonious relationship became stressful, and the children sensed the stress.

The effect on the children was dramatic. They complained about going from one household to the other. Christina and Ross each interpreted this as a function of the other parent's poor parenting skills, and the mistrust between them escalated. The older son became aggressive in school and had problems focusing and paying attention. The younger daughter seemed increasingly anxious and insecure, complaining of stomachaches when she knew her parents would see each other.

I held a marathon joint meeting with Christina, Ross, and all of their parents. I pointed out that both children had been happy and well adjusted before the financial wars but now were showing bad behavior and emotional reactions. Whenever one of the grandparents blamed the other, I repeated how the children told me how much they loved each of their parents and grandparents but knew the grandparents did not like each other. Ultimately both sets of grandparents agreed to leave the monthly child support issues to their children to work out and instead established equal college fund savings plans for the grandchildren.

When I saw Christina and Ross about a year later, the changes were noticeable. They were pleasant to each other and no longer fighting about money or schedules. The grandparents had funded college accounts, pleased their money was going to the grandchildren and not lawyers. The children were back to their happier selves.

Money issues are often stressors in marriage and can become overwhelmingly bitter in divorce. If you had trouble agreeing on those issues when you were married, just imagine how contentious they will be now that you both feel you are no longer beholden to the other. But therein lies the key: as co-parents you are still responsible to each other when it comes to one thing—your children. But it's so easy to forget that when the costs of such devotion start adding up.

And extended family and grandparents, fueled by anger, resentment, and especially fear of losing their grandchild, often fuel and fund the battle from afar.

For starters, divorce itself is expensive. Even in non-contentious situations, the direct cost of divorce can exceed $10,000. In highly contested divorces, legal fees alone can run $50,000 to $100,000 or more for each side. Then there are the costs of your new life: The cost of a second apartment or home, furnishings, an additional set of kitchenware, extra clothing and school supplies for the children, and, if you can afford it, two separate vacations—it all adds up quickly.

Now add to all that financial frustration the need to write a check to your ex. Even when it is intended to support the child you love, the act evokes anger and pain. On one level you know rationally that the money benefits your child. Nevertheless, the act of writing that check becomes a monthly misery. Parents required to pay child support would prefer writing a check to the Internal Revenue Service or giving a substantial donation to their least favorite charity. Either would be better than making out a monthly check to a hated ex.

Courts may order two different types of support payments postdivorce, and the propensity for awarding one or both varies by state. Spousal support or alimony may be awarded for a set number of years to compensate a parent for years of child-rearing work that took the parent out of the job market. Such support might also be used to allow time and training necessary to prepare the ex to return to the workforce. Child support is typically awarded based on the income of each parent. It is intended for the care and raising of the child, and usually remains in effect until the child is eighteen or graduates from high school. Child support covers the child's day-to-day expenses, including overhead costs for housing and utilities. Child support payments generally consider the child's lifestyle before the divorce, as well as the amount of time the child will live with each co-parent.

But complaints are quick to come from both sides as to how much child support should be given. One parent sees his ex's new car and wonders if that is where his child support money went. Another sees his ex remarry and knows her new spouse has the means to help support the child. Meanwhile, it gnaws that despite the divorce, even despite remarriage, the ex's finances remain co-mingled with your own. Of course, you want to buy food for your child, but knowing that he and your ex share a box of Cheerios makes you feel like you still buy your ex's food. She, on the other hand, thinks that his child support is miserly. She hates being beholden to her ex and controlled by him through his money. She yearns to be free of dependency. Yet she often needs that monthly check to make ends meet. She is most angry that he exerts control over how "her funds" are used, especially when he has no clue what jeans cost, nor that kids go through new shoes every few months, nor that only certain Nikes—this year's never-discounted model—are cool to wear to school.

In all cases, establishing clear financial expectations avoids conflicts about children's activities and costs. The child sees parents effectively communicating about needs and being respectful of each other. Your child doesn't have to worry about offending a parent by expressing any wants. Both parents have some "skin in the game"—a share of the costs—and are invested in making decisions based on the needs of their child.

Funding Your Co-Parenting

During their marriage, Rob and Jen constantly fought about money but resolved to be fair with each other after their separation. With the help of a parent coordinator, they established a financial plan for their daughter, Samantha. They agreed to pay for Samantha's expenses in proportion to their incomes and set an annual "Samantha budget." Each household bought its own games and toys and absorbed any expenses under $25. The parents used doctors in their insurance network to manage health expenses and alternated choosing extracurricular activities when they couldn't agree.

Jen did most of the driving and shopping. Monthly, she submitted

Samantha's expenses to Rob, who paid his portion within two weeks. Financial expectations were clear, and the parents dealt with expenses in a businesslike manner.

Rob and Jen did it right. Co-parents should establish a direct-deposit program by which funds automatically transfer on the first of each month from one account to the other. That way, one ex need never write a check to the other. Cost-of-living increases can be built into the account automatically by paying the bank a small fee to make annual adjustments. While the payer is certainly aware when funds flow out of one account and into the other, that ex need never actually put pen to paper to hand a check over to the other.

Computer software programs, such as Our Family Wizard (ourfamilywizard.com), allow parents to easily record child expenses and parent expenditures. Calendar features of the software give each parent full access to the child's schedule. Schedule changes are automatically emailed. All parental communications can be logged.

A second approach that also enables you to avoid writing your ex's name on a check is to establish a trust for the children. Talk to your banker about how to do this. The payer opens a separate bank account labeled "In trust for my children" and arranges for monthly deposits or transfers to "the custodial account of my children." Once the funds are deposited, the payee co-parent loses control over the funds. The other co-parent is named custodian of the account. That co-parent controls the funds exclusively for the benefit of the children. These monies pay for living expenses, food, health care, transportation, extracurriculars, and all other costs essential to the care of the child.

Since the payer loses control of the funds, use of the money falls within the discretion of the other co-parent. Theoretically, that co-parent could take the money and run—to the hairdresser, nail salon, or golf course—and the payer would have no knowledge of how the money was spent. That co-recipient need never justify to the payer how the funds were used.

The advantages of either of these mechanisms are clear: One ex no longer has to write that dreaded monthly check to the other. The other need not encounter each month that hated financial control, nor listen to a litany of excuses: "I forgot" . . . "I was out of town" . . . "The check is in the mail."

Most important, no longer will the child you love have to convey the monthly check to the ex you hate. By setting up a discrete financial system in advance, the co-parents shelter the child from their anger over financial matters. Your child is free to love both parents and will not be involved in the parent money business.

Ultimately, of course, whether or not your child gets the new Nikes you are arguing about is not as damaging as the actual fighting between the parents. If your child sees a healthy parenting relationship and you can demonstrate respectful financial decision making, your child will model your positive behavior.

Separate the business of co-parenting from the business of financing the child.

CHAPTER 4

Together Again — Sort of: From Holidays to Soccer Games

James, age twelve, had alternating weekend living arrangements with Mom and Dad. While married, his parents had encouraged his physical skills and directed them toward soccer. Following his parents' divorce, the issue of who was responsible for James's soccer training became contentious. Dad was "drafted" to be an assistant coach after the regular coach moved on to a travel soccer league. Mom then protested that Dad got to see his son on noncustodial soccer Saturdays and during weeknight practices when he did not have visitations. He had exceeded his custodial boundaries and violated their agreement. Mom even sent letters, with a copy of the court order, to the soccer league commissioner to prove that Dad was violating the court order on practice nights. This put the league commissioner in a bind. She had no idea what else she could do other than to ask Dad to stop coaching. Both parents continued to attend all of James's games, but, of course, James felt his parents' hostility.

Meanwhile, the other soccer parents were understandably furious that James's mom had cost them a valuable soccer coach. They went out of their way to include Dad, his new wife, and their new baby as they huddled together on the sidelines. Mom, aware of her rejection and needing to avoid Dad and his new family, took up her post in no-man's-land behind the goalposts.

James was all too well aware of the situation on his home team's sideline and his mother's out-sideline. Quickly, his performance in games deteriorated. In practices he continued to show great skill and promise, but during games he just could not deliver. Mom blamed Dad for pushing James so hard. Dad blamed Mom for forcing him out as coach. James was trapped. If he played well and scored, he would please Dad and alienate Mom. If he played poorly, his mother felt vindicated and his father was disappointed.

When I first met James for consultation because of some trouble at school, he told me he had severe allergies to grasses and pollen. Neither parent had mentioned that during our initial intake interview, but when questioned, both said that James had recently started complaining of sneezing and wheezing. Testing by an allergist found only weak seasonal allergies that had probably been present for years. Yet now James began waking up on Saturday mornings complaining that he was congested. He started taking over-the-counter antihistamines, but they left him too groggy to play soccer. James had—as so often children will—masterfully figured out how to avoid the stressful situation. He would no longer play soccer, presumably not because of parental conflict but rather for medical reasons. James, keenly cognizant of the tension between his parents, had fixed the problem himself—but in so doing, he had abandoned something he loved to do.

With parent coordination (a process discussed later in this book), the parents agreed to alternate attending James's games. Mom agreed to sit on the sidelines with the rest of the team's parents, even if she would not be in the middle of their social activities as Dad was. Both parents promised to tell James how much they wanted him to enjoy himself. Within three weeks, his "allergies" had cleared, and James was back to focusing on his game rather than shouldering the responsibility for circumventing his parents' anger.

Showing Up at the Games

As a rule, neither parent should be held back from attending significant events in the life of the child. At best, co-parenting agreements list a range of very broad activities—religious, educational, cultural, athletic, and extracurricular—that parents must agree upon. They rarely discuss the issue of parents' attending those events.

Both parents do not typically show up for an entire season's worth of baseball practices for a thirteen-year-old. Instead they usually just provide transportation. So there would be no reason for the Tuesday noncustodial parent to attend those practices. However, not only are both parents likely to attend league playoff championships, but, regardless of custodial arrangements, grandparents, stepparents, stepsiblings, and extended family members will also likely show up. All should be welcome at such important moments in the life of your child, no matter who has custody for those few hours.

However, managing attendance at the fourteen regular-season games is a far greater concern. Some co-parents leave it open-ended: the physical custodial parent—the one in charge of that Saturday—is responsible for transporting the child to and from the game. The non-physical custodial parent may attend if she wishes. Other families try to reduce the potential for conflict: the co-parent deliberately attends only the games that fall on her physical custody days.

When the noncustodial parent attends an event, she should respect the rights of her ex. She has shown up to only support and encourage her child. Her presence demonstrates that both parents care deeply about the child's activities. The exes must try to adhere to a business model at these events. If this were a business exchange, such as those between officers of competing firms, you would greet your opponent politely and exchange a few meaningless pleasantries. The exes' conversation should similarly be banal and mundane: "Hello, Cheryl, how are you?" "Fine, Robert, how are you?" No more is called for. The non-physical custodial parent should also greet the child, if appropriate, with a kiss and a hug and then make only the briefest of comments about the upcoming event: "Have a great game." The parent can also add something like "I'm so proud of your _____ (name the accomplishment: winning a trophy, getting inducted into the Spanish Honor society)."

This is not the time to check if the child took his medication, finished his homework, wanted a playdate for the next weekend when he is with you, or left something he needed for next weekend at his mom's. Respond appropriately to the child but don't initiate detailed conversations. If the child brags, "Hey Dad, I got a 96 on my math test," say: "Great job! We knew you could do it." But if the child does not volunteer information, do not start grilling him about his math test or commenting about your ex's lifestyle. When Dad snarls: "I am glad your mother got you here on time for once," he suggests the mother's failures and needlessly adds tension. The central rule to remember is: these events are moments for your child to score points on the field, not for you to score points against your ex.

Parents need not sit near each other at the game (or in the church pew), but they should stay in the same general vicinity on the sidelines. I want James looking at his defender and his goalpost, figuring out a way to score—not scanning one sideline looking for Mom and the other looking for Dad.

After the game your child must feel free to greet both parents. Think of the situation from your child's point of view: how awkward it is for him to shuttle in front of his teammates from sideline to sideline to say hi to Mom and then to Dad. After the game, all of the other players and parents converge to hear the coaches' feedback, to congratulate or to commiserate with one another, and to have snacks. Do not make your child feel different because you don't want to join in the post-game camaraderie. Remember, you were married to your ex for years. Together you produced this child. Surely, as individuals who agreed to co-parent, you can manage for just a few minutes to stand within ten feet of each other and jointly congratulate your child and his teammates on what they have accomplished.

This is a soccer game, not a contest for your child's affection. You need not keep score of which parent, stepparent, or sibling your child greets first or longest. If you do not ascribe any greater meaning to your child's interactions with other members of his family, your child will be able to focus on what is important—the game he just played and how he played it.

If you are the noncustodial parent that day, congratulate your child and teammates on a well-played game. Do not use this time to teach your child lifelong lessons. Do say: "Your team's defense looked great today." Do not preach: "Just look at how our hard work and all those practices in our backyard paid off."

The noncustodial parent should leave first, to save the child the awkwardness of a separate and sad good-bye. Say: "Great game. Have a good week. I love you. See you next Wednesday." Then give a hug—and be off.

Be courteous to your ex as you leave, just as you would in any business exchange. "The kids looked good out there. Have a nice week." This suffices for now, even if you already plan to argue later that week about child support and vacation dates. In front of your child, on that soccer field, before his teammates and their families, do not start an argument, exchange clothes, discuss health insurance forms, or review the week's schedule. All of these should be done off the playing field of your child's life. Following these guidelines will guarantee that both parents may participate and take pride in the future significant events in your child's life.

Sharing the Love—Handling the Holidays

There are several different approaches to managing holidays and significant events in the lives of children. Sometimes parents alternate years—Thanksgiving with Father on even-numbered years and with Mother on odd-numbered years. For others, if the child spends Thanksgiving with Father, then she spends Christmas Day with Mother that year. Other times, parents prefer to divide up the significant days—Thanksgiving with Mother until 3:00 p.m. and then with Father after 3:00 p.m. This allows the child to celebrate each holiday with both families. To ensure that domestic law attorneys remain well employed in interpreting documents, the two approaches are sometimes combined, alternating years and alternating times—that is, in odd-numbered years the father has the children on Thanksgiving from 10:00 a.m. until 3:00 p.m.; after 3:00 p.m. they go to Mother. For even-numbered years the mother has the children on Thanksgiving day from 10:00 a.m. until 3:00 p.m.; Father has them during odd-numbered years the opposite times. Yet a third approach, especially popular with parents of younger children, may be to try to spend holidays and other special times together, believing that maintaining family traditions is better for their children.

In examining which approach might be the best for the child, let's go back to our key foundational factors: the child's perception of a consistent and meaningful relationship with both parents, the ability of the co-parents to make parenting decisions together, and their capacity to eliminate, as much as possible, parental conflict perceived by the child.

First, let's take a hypothetical look at the concept of the co-parents coming together for the holidays. Trying to "ease" the children into the divorce, the family starts out by agreeing to share in their son Sean's fifth birthday party. Theoretically this is a wonderful idea, but in reality, it often makes for disaster.

Where will the party be held? Not at Mom's house: Dad has too many negative and uncomfortable associations with it. Not at Dad's new condo: that is too far away from where Sean's classmates live. Having the party at a neutral site, like the Gymboree Center or a local roller-skating rink, may not be what Sean wants and is surely an unexpected extra expense at a time when finances are already impacted by the costs of divorce and setting up two households.

Even if the co-parents manage to agree on a site, how comfortable will they be at the party? And more important, how will Sean feel? Family members who took sides in the divorce now have to smile at the ex they hate. And didn't Sean already tell everyone that his mommy and daddy don't like each other anymore and that they are no longer living in the same house? What will his friends say to him when they see Sean's mom and dad celebrating his birthday together? Meanwhile Sean's parents have to deal with real or imagined smirks and gossip from his friends' parents who are trying to get the scoop on their divorce.

That's just for starters. Then there's the heavy-duty emotional baggage that comes with experiencing an important life event together. Sean's parents may be thinking of the day he was born and of how different their relationship had been at that time. During the party she may wonder if her ex was already cheating on her back then. He may think: "Even if we pull it off for this year, even if both sets of grandparents manage not to glare at each other for Sean's sake, what will happen next year? My new girlfriend's children, who play with Sean, already feel slighted that they were not invited." She thinks: "What will happen when my new boyfriend wants to join in next year's party?" Meanwhile, Sean is caught in the middle, wondering which side of the room to smile at first as he opens his presents while each parent tries to capture the moment on separate digital cameras.

Is it fair to make Sean uncomfortable on his birthday? If both his parents manage to smile this year, will Sean fantasize that he has the power to bring them back together? Sean will plot: "Since they were so happy at my birthday party, I can see that they still like each other. I'll find other times for them to get together. Then they will get married again." Sharing birthdays and significant events sounds like a good idea, but it is difficult to implement practically over time.

The Middle Ground for Your Child

Often what seems fair and logical to the exes does not appear that way to the child. For example, splitting a holiday seems reasonable to the co-parents: One family has its big Thanksgiving meal at lunch, the other at dinner. This way the child can see all his cousins, family, and friends from both sides of his family on the same day. He also gets two special meals and two desserts. But from the child's perspective, her parents have introduced another transition—a change in both the physical and psychological space for the child, where the child goes from being in the care of one parent to being in the care of the other. And transitions are pretty tough on children after a divorce.

All transitions entail three stages: preparation, the moment of actual transition, and post-transition adjustment. Parental agreements tend to focus on the actual transition, often with great specificity. "Mother shall pick up Sean from father's house at 3:00 p.m. Thanksgiving Days in even-numbered years. She shall not enter the father's household, but shall call the father on his cellular or land-base line five minutes before 3:00 p.m. so that the child will exit father's house to be picked up by the mother." While the warring exes want specificity for the physical transition, the actual moment of transition is likely the least worrisome of the three stages for children like Sean. Assuming his parents are behaving as co-parents and are civil, appropriate, and distantly polite, Sean is not really worried about the actual transition. Instead, preparing to transition and the post-transition adjustment are far more sensitive for him. Sean prepares to transition by wrapping up his activities at his mom's house. He is the one who must leave Thanksgiving lunch early. His cousins are heading out to play football in the street, but he needs to get his stuff together to go to his dad's. Sure, it is great to get dessert twice, but Sean also knows his dad's mom will be upset if he does not eat what she has cooked, so he had better not eat too much at Mom's Thanksgiving lunch. He also needs to think about what he has to take with him. He is off from school for a few days, so that means he should bring his Game Boy. But he does have some homework, so that means he'd better pack his books in his backpack. Sean knows that when he gets to his dad's house, everyone will be waiting for him. Since the divorce he has really tried to avoid being the center of attention, and this will make him very uncomfortable. Focusing on the upcoming transition makes Sean anxious and adds tension to his holiday.

The post-transition adjustment is also difficult. It's hard for Sean to leave Mom's house on Thanksgiving Day, having to say good-bye to all the family there, then to spend twenty minutes in the car with Dad, whom he has not seen for several days, and then to walk into his grandmother's house. In the best circumstances, it takes a child a short while to adjust from one house to the other. In regularly occurring transitions, the parents expect the period of adjustment and give the child the space and time needed. However, on a holiday or special occasion, the schedule is so tight that each parent maximizes time with the child and his extended family, and the child has to give up on the routines that have previously helped him ease these transitions.

Other co-parents favor the option of rotating years for holidays, but this also has pitfalls. Frankly, it is just hard for the child not to see both parents to celebrate birthdays, Christmas, Thanksgiving, and other occasions customarily spent with both families. Spending Christmas week with Dad because it is an odd-numbered year may work for the parents, but it ignores the needs of the child. Not seeing Mom at any time during the Christmas holiday leaves the child feeling empty and hollow. A pre-scheduled phone call to Mom on Christmas morning and getting her boatload of presents is great, but spending Christmas away from Mom entirely because it is Dad's year to have the child simply underscores the split in the family.

When children are asked if there is anything good about parental separation, they usually give two positive responses. One is that Mom and Dad don't fight with each other as much anymore; the other is that "now I will get double birthday and holiday presents." Children of divorce have experienced trauma and loss; the short-term pleasure of having two birthday parties, one at Daddy's and one at Mommy's, may seem inconsequential to adults, but it does provide some small consolation to the child and probably a reduction of pain and trauma.

Most children already have their birthday parties on a weekend, so it makes sense for the child of divorce to have two different birthday celebrations, one with one parent one weekend and with the other the following weekend. Obviously, the parties cannot be the same: One might be a large party with clowns and entertainment for thirty kids from the child's class. The other is a smaller but no less special celebration with just two or three close friends doing something fun like going skating and out to a favorite restaurant afterward. From the child's perspective, this system decreases the pressure of the transitions, and he gets two parties.

Just as with the birthday parties, let Sean spend all of Thanksgiving at one parent's house, and then have a second Thanksgiving celebration at the other the next day. Alternating years so that every other year each family celebrates the holiday on its assigned day allows Sean to experience each holiday fully with each parent, and having Thanksgiving on Fridays also creates a new holiday tradition for Sean's family.

4: TOGETHER AGAIN—SORT OF: FROM HOLIDAYS TO SOCCER GAMES

Christmas is often the most emotionally charged holiday to divide, yet it has the built-in dividing line of Christmas Eve and Christmas Day. Let the child spend one with one parent and one with the other. This does mean that every other year one co-parent is not there to see the child open gifts on Christmas morning, but the family can develop a new tradition by opening gifts Christmas Eve before the child leaves at 10:00 p.m. to go to his other home, to spend the night and awaken to celebrations the next morning.

The key is flexibility and responsiveness to the child. The decisions made during separation will likely not be the same decisions you want five years from now. Most parents do a good job describing their child's current needs and behavior but fail when they try to predict their child's future needs.

Changing life circumstances, moves, new relationships, conflicting family demands—all require both parents to be open to creatively adapting their custody agreement to adjust to family changes.

If you want to ensure the health of your child, then agree to be flexible when it comes to family gatherings, and convey that agreement to the child: "I hope you really enjoy seeing your cousins at your dad's house Friday night for Thanksgiving dinner." The child then is able to maintain a consistent and meaningful relationship with both parents, perceives that his parents both make important decisions about his life, and sees limited conflict between his parents after separation and divorce.

CHAPTER 5

Everyday Matters: School and Religion

Allison was a fifteen-year-old high school student whose parents divorced when she was five. Both parents remarried, and she had stepsiblings from her mother and her father. She had resided primarily with her father during the summers and with her mother during the school year, but every year around springtime Father still requested formally and informally that Allison come live with him and his family during the school week.

A straight-A, gifted and talented student, Allison strenuously resisted going to live with Father, because she didn't want to switch to the school in his neighborhood. And she came to dread the annual ritual of Father's request and the co-parent conflict that invariably ensued.

So when it came time for high school, her parents crafted a compromise: Allison would apply to the County Magnet Gifted and Talented Program. Its school was physically closer to Father's house and would allow Allison to spend a few of her school days at her father's.

But when Allison was rejected from the magnet high school program, her parents' willingness to work together quickly disintegrated. Mother simply enrolled Allison in her neighborhood high school. Father quickly rented a condo near the county's academically strongest high school, where Allison would be eligible for many advanced placement courses. Now, he argued, Allison's educational needs would best be met in his local school. "His" high school had more advanced placement classes, smaller class size, a wider range of electives, more experienced and qualified teachers, higher SAT scores, a higher rate of college acceptance, more county-wide honor students, more diverse athletic choices, and a wider range of extracurricular activities. It was clear from the twenty-plus pages of spreadsheets Father presented documenting this data that "his" school was a better choice for a gifted student like Allison. However, his data ignored two crucial factors: Allison's friends were all in the school near her mother's house, and she was happier there.

Choosing the school your child will attend is often one of the most difficult and potentially divisive decisions in co-parenting. Adults who have acted in a civil manner throughout the entire divorce proceedings, who have successfully reached agreement on living arrangements and legal decision making, who figured out effective means of communication, and who settled property issues as if they were Wall Street money managers, can deteriorate into aggressive, selfish devils when school placement decisions come up.

But school is one of the most basic and central parts of a child's life. When deciding on an issue that so directly affects the child's core world, both co-parents must forget about what they want and realize that parental separation causes intense changes for their child. The structure of his home, daily routine, bedtime, and level of responsibility within the household has changed dramatically and overnight. Therefore, it is

5: EVERYDAY MATTERS: SCHOOL AND RELIGION

paramount, especially during the first year or two post-divorce, to retain the maximum possible "normalcy," and that means a life as close as possible to the pattern of the child's life before the divorce.

Since your child's school is one of the most "normal" patterns she has, I recommend that for the first year or two following parental separation/divorce, you do whatever you can to keep your child in her current school—period. Regardless of all the reasons why you might think a change would do her good, keep your child in the school system she attended before your separation for at least the remainder of the academic year and, if at all possible, for the next. Even if the divorce forces you to move, most school systems allow the child to finish the school year at the base home school. You may then petition the school system to permit the child to stay for another year, arguing that her emotional needs require the stability of staying at the same school.

That's a pretty valid argument, because schools are far more than just educational settings. In effect, your child's school is his and your community center. He benefits from the familiarity of staying in his regular school, hanging out with his old friends, and attending his usual after-school programs. The school offers the co-parents and their child the companionship of social networks and opportunities for growth and expression. Here your child takes art and drama classes on weekends. On its fields and in its gyms, he plays ball. On its playgrounds, he meets his friends. Playdates, soccer leagues, baseball teams, Boy Scouts, and Cub Scout troops form out of classroom cohorts. Powerful parental connections and friendships develop too, relationships that directly and indirectly add to your child's feeling of stability.

While you or your spouse might think that a new school system, new teacher, new school routine, new friends, and new classroom dynamics are just what your child needs for a "fresh start," you must, if at all possible, avoid another great disruption in your child's life. And although staying in the same school may add stress to your lives as parents, this arrangement is better for the child, and co-parenting demands that both of you must make these accommodations for the sake of the child's emotional stability. It is simply and inarguably the right thing to do if at all possible.

Choosing a New School If You Must

But it's not always possible to do so. Often it's not just the selfish desires of the parents or even the well-intentioned plan to have your child in the "best" school that gets in the way of that normalcy, but rather real-world challenges. Because divorce so frequently leads to significant social and economic changes for one or both co-parents, often they have no choice but to force a change. Before the divorce, the parents could together afford a home in a particular school district. Now, after the divorce, that house may need to be sold, and neither co-parent can afford to buy a new home in the old neighborhood. Hence they both move, and their child must find a new school.

If the divorce necessitates moving to a new school system, try to do it at a time of natural transition. Preschool to kindergarten, elementary to middle school, and middle to high school are points of natural change when your child would be jumping into a new school in any system. At these times, schools—and likely the new entering class—become melting pots, absorbing students from different settings. The goal following parental separation is to minimize the numbers and types of transitions for the child. Separation and divorce are such major disturbances that avoiding all other disruptions as much as possible—especially the shift from one school to another—is the parents' objective.

In an ideal situation, the two parents should live within the same school district. When both parents find homes in the same school district, they can each claim ownership of the school. But this ideal is rarely practical. When parents divorce and move, one of the co-parents' new neighborhoods will "win out" over the other by becoming the primary base for the child's life outside the home. In a disproportionate weekday living arrangement, where the child lives more school days with one parent than with the other, meeting the child's needs usually means sending him to the school closest to his primary home. Or in a living arrangement where the child divides her time equally between two homes, other factors, such as the best options for after-school care, may become decision makers about which school the child will attend.

For some co-parents, the question of "owning" the school is resolved by having the child attend a private or parochial school in a neighborhood that is neutral to both co-parents but near a natural transition point. The private school thus becomes the community for both co-parents. Here each forms his or her own network of connections and friends.

But whichever of the new school options you decide best suits your child, that decision should be based on what each educational system offers to meet your child's needs, the ease of transportation to the schools, and any special extracurriculars your child may pursue at school. This is about the child—not about you.

In choosing a school, the needs of the child should be of paramount consideration. The child with a significant learning disability needs a school offering disability resources; these can range from individual tutoring to a self-contained classroom. The gifted and talented child will succeed best in a school system with strong academics. For a gifted athlete, you should consider a school with a strong athletic program in addition to its curriculum. Though relationships with stepsiblings are certainly important, they should not factor into choosing a school. Parents in blended families will often argue for the child to attend school with her stepsiblings. But this argument is more often about the convenience of the co-parent in the blended family—who desires to arrange transportation to only one school and coordinate playdates for multiple children in one neighborhood—than it is about the welfare of the child. The divorced child needs to develop her own sense of connections to the school she attends. The child's needs—to maintain a sense of stability, to have her educational needs fully met, and to attend a school accessible to both her parents—far outweigh the convenience of the co-parent who wants his children and stepchildren in the same school district.

Home schooling should rarely be initiated after divorce. To initiate home schooling following divorce is deeply problematic, since it takes the child out of the school he knew and trusted and also completely excludes one parent from the child's educational process. As noted previously, it is imperative for parents to maintain as much stability as possible for the child following separation and divorce. If your child has been home schooled all along, then, of course, continue. If not, this is not the time to start.

New School: Parental Adjustment Required

You may feel socially disconnected from the school and neighborhood. You may feel you lose power because it is "Mom's school" and that she has friends there, not you. But remember: that school holds an important key to your child's stability, and that key outweighs your feelings about being an outsider in that school.

If you do not live in the same school district as your child, you need to make a concerted effort to join this community. The best way to do that is by volunteering. Offer to be a room parent; join any one of the many committees of the parent/teacher organization; coordinate the weekly computer animé club; agree to become the assistant soccer coach for the extracurricular team formed by several children in your child's class. These involvements are those of a parent; they in no way interfere with the life of your ex—unless, of course, you both choose to volunteer for the same project, a situation that should be avoided.

Your involvements in these school and extracurricular settings make you a part of the central backdrop of your child's life. Now, even though you do not live in this community, your child's friends and their parents come to know you. If you are the softball coach, your child's friends' parents will be unlikely to balk at driving twenty minutes to your house for a weekend sleepover.

The child's play, social, and athletic activities become based in this school and its environs. The parents in a co-parenting arrangement should be equally involved in the child's school activities. Both co-parents can easily remain actively involved. But remember: the key here is to not disrupt the child's routine. That means that on the weeks when you do not have physical custody, do not drop in at the school to have lunch with your child as a way of circumventing limitations on the time when you may see your child. However, if you do not have to work on Wednesday afternoons and the kindergarten teacher wants parents to volunteer in the classroom, then, by all means, volunteer. The teacher needs the extra pair of hands, and whether this time falls within your physical custody or that of your ex will not matter to your child and should not matter to your ex.

Both co-parents should attend special school events, regardless of who has physical custody that day. In good co-parenting arrangements, both parents actively participate in meaningful events in the life of the child. Thus, both parents should be there for school plays, holiday pageants, and even on Dr. Seuss's birthday for Read across America. Both parents should buy the candy and gift wrap for the school fund-raisers. However, do not turn these purchases into a competition to see which parent spends more. Successful co-parenting is not a competitive sport.

Declaring the school neutral territory where the exes agree not to do battle incorporates co-parenting's three cardinal rules. School becomes a setting where both parents can become active in the day-to-day life of their child. When both exes attend teacher conferences, special school events, and performances, the child sees both Mom and Dad not only focused on her life, but doing so without conflict. School becomes a place where your child sees both parents he loves making decisions important to his life.

When thinking about the child's school placement during separation and after divorce, the ground rules are: Any and all changes must meet the needs of the child, not the needs of his parents. Try to keep the child in the same school for one to two years post-divorce. When the child must switch school systems, make the change at a natural transition point. Consider a "neutral" private or parochial school if that is financially feasible and if it helps to avoid competition between the co-parents championing their respective neighborhood schools. Finally, both parents need to get involved in the school. The educational and social needs of the child come first.

Matters of Faith

Richard and Monica were both raised in moderately religious homes, though in different faiths. He went to Hebrew school for the requisite number of years before having a bar mitzvah at thirteen, after which he was no longer pressured to attend services. Monica attended Sunday school irregularly with her mother and older sister until her older sister rebelled when Monica was ten. Attendance at church became more sporadic after that.

Religious differences were not relevant to Richard and Monica when they dated after college. They shared common suburban experiences that made them comfortable with each other. Neither of their fathers cared much about the religion question, and both mothers extracted from their children vague promises that grandchildren, a far-flung thought at that time, would be raised in their respective faiths.

Richard and Monica seriously addressed the religious questions as they spoke of marriage. Both felt that organized religion had failed to meet their needs, but family-based holiday celebrations were important. They pledged to show respect for both faiths, to allow their children a smattering of education in each, and to observe with their extended families holiday meals and gatherings. They agreed that when their children reached adolescence, they would decide their own religious beliefs just as Richard and Monica had done. Monica vaguely promised that if the children wanted bar mitzvahs they could have them, thinking mostly of the parties she had attended for Jewish friends in middle school and not focused on the actual religious training and services. Richard thought a small Christmas tree would be fine and looked forward to not feeling "left out on Christmas."

All went according to plan after their son, Jordan, was born, and religious practice played a minimal part in their lives. They considered having Jordan attend a neighborhood preschool at the local temple because of its top-rated education, but chose a different preschool based on schedule, cost, and convenience. They ecumenically celebrated major holidays in their homes, putting up a Christmas tree and lighting Hanukkah candles. They visited grandparents for Easter and Passover. Monica took Jordan to Christmas Mass and sometimes Richard would take Jordan to Yom Kippur services.

It was truly an exercise in religious tolerance and respect until the couple decided to divorce for completely unrelated reasons. Suddenly what seemed like a perfect compromise with Jordan's best interests at heart exploded into a religious tug-of-war with their son caught in the middle.

At first it seemed as if Richard and Monica had a relatively amicable divorce, using a mediator to agree on financial matters and establish joint legal custody, with both parents needing to agree on "health, education, extracurricular activities, summer plans, and religious and moral training of their child."

But tensions increased between Richard and Monica when Jordan was ten and both sets of grandparents began to pressure for more religious training in their respective faiths. Monica's parents wanted Jordan in confirmation classes, and Richard's mother was pushing for Sunday sessions in preparation for bar mitzvah.

Monica objected to the whole bar mitzvah preparation. Although she acknowledged agreeing earlier that their child would have a bar mitzvah, she thought that merely meant he would go to services and have a party celebrating the thirteenth birthday. Monica was not willing to give up her every other Sunday morning with Jordan so he could go to Hebrew school, asking Richard how he would feel if she decided to go to church with Jordan every Sunday morning. And she certainly wasn't going to agree to private bar mitzvah instruction one night a week. She told Richard that she would not object to the bar mitzvah, but she would not modify her schedule, give up her time, or drive regularly for lessons. Monica agreed to tell Jordan to study his bar mitzvah lessons while at her home "if time permitted," after he finished his homework and "other activities." But of course, she could not help him.

Different principles of their custody agreement were at conflict. One—"neither parent shall make plans that infringe on the time of the other parent"—suggests that Richard could not sign Jordan up for Sunday bar mitzvah lessons because they conflicted with Monica's Sundays. Even if Richard picked Jordan up, drove him, and arranged for Monica to have other times with Jordan, Richard couldn't make plans without Monica's consent for Jordan to regularly do things when Jordan was with his mother. A second principle—each parent "needs to actively support the parenting decision of the other parent"—suggests that the significant life event of the bar mitzvah should be actively supported by Monica. Verbal agreements made by the parents ten years earlier were of limited standing. Each had a different perspective on what was meant, and without a prenuptial contract that delineated the terms of their agreement, that discussion was of limited validity.

Meanwhile their son, Jordan, seemingly gave different responses to each of his parents as to what he wanted. To his father he said he would not mind having a party with friends and family. To his mother he said no way was he giving up his hockey games on Sundays to learn Hebrew. Jordan actually was consistent: he was telling each parent what he thought each wanted to hear. Essentially his parent's tug-of-war was going on inside his head, too.

When principles of co-parenting conflict, compromise cannot be reached, and a negative impact on the child is being evidenced, creative, alternative solutions have to be found, which is eventually what happened in this case. Richard found a private tutor willing to give Jordan lessons on an every-other-week basis. The bar mitzvah would not be held in the temple, but the social hall being considered for the celebratory party had a wedding type of chapel that could easily be used as a sanctuary. The tutor helped Richard and his family write a personalized bar mitzvah service, and Jordan chanted the ancient prayers in a ceremony attended by friends and family. Monica was ultimately supportive of Jordan practicing at her house and participated with appropriate readings at her son's bar mitzvah. As Jordan saw his parents develop a meaningful alternative, his tension eased.

Co-parenting means you are not always going to get what you want. But you need to remember this isn't about you; it's about your child. And when dealing with aspects of your child's life and world that are so central to his being and routines, some decisions may seem unreasonable to you. However, you no longer control the values, schooling, or religious and moral upbringing of your child all the time. These are shared in a business partnership with someone you once loved but now do not. Your ex may seem unbending and unsupportive. But as with Richard and Monica, creative solutions can lead to compromise. Other times one parent will not get his or her needs met. But you are trying to create for your child as stable, harmonious, and conflict-free a world as you can.

Changes in schools and religious activities can create difficult adjustments for both parents and children. Maintain as much stability as you can, but remember you will not always get everything you want.

Part Two

WHAT IF . . .
CO-PARENTING THE UNEXPECTED,
AND INEVITABLE, SITUATIONS

CHAPTER 6

Introducing New People into Your Child's Life

Mr. White was a charming, narcissistic philanderer who disliked birth control and avoided using it whenever possible. In college he had briefly married the girlfriend he got pregnant. By the time he met Mrs. White, he had three children from two different relationships and was responsible for child support for all three. However, he maintained a minimal relationship with only one child; he never saw the others.

When he swept Mrs. White off her feet, he somehow neglected to tell her about his children. She discovered them only after lawyer letters and angry phone calls came when he failed to pay child support. But by then, Mr. White's family finances were constrained. Mrs. White had become pregnant right away, and then he had David—and now Billy—to take care of, too.

Soon the marriage began to show strain. Mr. White had affairs. Mrs. White got angrier. When Mr. White came home with a sexually transmitted disease, Mrs. White moved out.

Mr. White demanded that his sons, now ages eight and seven, live with him enough of the time so that, as an effective co-parent, his child support payments to Mrs. White would be limited. At first, the boys had regular visitations with their father, but very soon they became sporadic. Visitations on weekend nights ceased. Mr. White said he had to work weekends or blamed Mrs. White for not sending the right clothes or games for their overnights. Within a few months of separation, Mr. White was no longer taking the boys over to the apartment he had rented near the family home so that he could co-parent. Mr. White would take his sons out to dinner occasionally, but he returned them to their mother's place afterward. One weekend, Mother was ill. Desperate, she asked Mr. White to take the children. He refused.

Meanwhile, the boys began hearing about Miss Sally, Daddy's special friend, whom they could not meet because "Mommy's bitch of a lawyer" wouldn't allow it. Of course, Mr. White had never discussed with Mrs. White his plan to introduce Miss Sally to their sons. Not only was Mr. White telling the boys about "the mysterious Miss Sally," but he was also hinting how wonderful it would be if they had a baby brother. Mrs. White, just six months separated from Mr. White, put two and two together. She found Mr. White living with a coworker who was seven months pregnant. Having no idea how to act on what she now knew, Mrs. White never confronted Mr. White. She hoped this new relationship would play itself out as had the others whose children he had abandoned.

But it didn't. Two months later while eating with his sons in a Burger King, Mr. White told David and Billy that they had a new baby brother whom they needed to love and that Miss Sally, whom they had never met, was their new stepmother. Father told his sons that they would meet their new baby brother and Miss Sally on Friday, and that from now on, they would spend every other weekend with Father and his new family. There was just one small problem, which even an eight-year-old could figure out: the Whites were separated, not divorced. David asked his mother how could Daddy get married and have a new baby when he was still married to her. Not surprisingly, Mrs. White did not know what to say.

You Love Him, You Love Her: When Should They Meet?

After the hell of separation and divorce, the yelling and screaming, the fights over what is right for the kids, the fortune you handed over to your lawyers, your own financial downward trend, and all the doubts and self-blame, you swear you will never get involved with anyone again. But guess what? You do. Whether before, during, or after the time when your marriage disintegrates, you are likely to meet someone new, someone so different from—or maybe the same as—the ex you loathe that you jump headfirst into a new relationship. How wonderful: you have someone new and important in your life. Or is it?

The fact is that most divorced people date and remarry, some within five years, others within ten. You hope one day to find yourself in a new relationship, but don't put that before the welfare of your child.

When the co-parent gets into a new relationship, the first question to ask and answer candidly is: What comes first? Co-parenting the children you want to guide to maturity or the overpowering lust and love of a new relationship? If the honest answer is that overpowering new relationship, then you should not expect to do much co-parenting. Separation and divorce are traumatic. That is why the phrase "rebound relationship" exists. If you are co-parenting your children, back off from a new relationship until the old one is settled. A new relationship is not good for you, and it is certainly, at this time, bad for your children. It is best not to become involved in any new serious relationship for the first year following separation.

And once you do begin that new relationship, you don't necessarily need to let your son or daughter know about it. Honesty is not the best policy here, but rather discretion. Here's why.

Your divorce agreement reads: "Neither parent will expose the child to a relationship with a non-blood relative of the opposite sex with whom there is a personal, intimate relationship until that relationship is significant." Great, you are glad to have covered that in your agreement. But what does it mean? I can guarantee you that you and your ex will interpret this clause differently. You will call a relationship significant; your ex will not. You will assert about your new significant other: "We are careful not to be intimate on the weekends I have our child; therefore, I am not violating the agreement." One father actually boasted to me that it was just fine for his eight-year-old son to meet a revolving cast of girlfriends, because he just had sex with them; there was nothing personal and intimate about these relationships.

But you are finding that you get to see your new boyfriend only when your child is with your ex, but your ex is, as he always was, unreliable. Sometimes he is late; sometimes she has a business trip and at the last minute cannot take the child. Your ex is ruining your social life and impeding your new relationship. And also you think, before this relationship gets too serious, that you want your kids to check out your new friend. So if your son absolutely hates your new lover or if your new friend is just a jerk with your daughter, you can end this relationship now. You know not to sleep with your girlfriend in front of your child; you just want to stop hiding. You want your child to see you happy and to trust you again. You think, "After my dysfunctional marriage, it is good for my child to see a healthy relationship." It is so easy to convince yourself that you have your child's best interest at heart.

6: INTRODUCING NEW PEOPLE INTO YOUR CHILD'S LIFE

But the truth is that you don't—unless the relationship is serious and likely to be around for a long run. Not until then is it time for your child to meet your lover. Just as this event is significant for you, so too it is a momentous occasion for your child.

One real benefit of co-parenting is that you do get time off from your child. You can enjoy a social life away from his prying eyes. I know you want to share your new happiness and to show him: "See, Daddy's not such a jerk after all. He has a good-looking, sweet girlfriend. So he can't be the bastard Mommy makes him out to be." But think of your child, not of yourself, and spare him. Tell your friends instead. They like you; it's their job to acknowledge, validate, and vindicate you. These are not appropriate roles for your child.

Your child also has no need to meet your dates, which may, at first, come in the form of the flavor of the month. When you are reasonably sure that this is a relationship of meaning and permanency, then they should meet. Until then, when your child asks if you are dating, do not lie. Respond with the truth, but spare her details that, depending on her age, are either beyond her comprehension or unnecessary for her to know. Say: "Yes, I sometimes go out to dinner with friends when you are with your dad." That will suffice for most children. It is the truth. They do not need to know about the romantic dinners you have been having over the past six weeks.

You must understand that your breaking the news about your new partner shatters your child's fantasy that somehow he is going to see his parents reunite. Since your divorce, your child has seesawed back and forth between trying to please you when he is with you and working to get you and your ex back together. There is a reason the movie *The Parent Trap* was so popular. Children of divorce think that if only they could magically do something, they could get Mommy and Daddy back together again. Now you announce that you are dating someone else. There goes his pipe dream. Not only do most pre-adolescent and many early adolescent children think parental dating is gross, but the news that you are seriously dating someone has just smashed his dream.

Your new relationship also poses a direct risk to the quality and quantity of the time your child will spend only with you. Other than double birthday presents, one-on-one time with each parent is one of the few perks the child gets out of a divorce. When you were married, parents and children did things together, even the fighting, as a noisy family. In the swirl of school, work, and activities, you probably did not spend much time focused solely on your child. But since your divorce, you and your child have had evenings and weekends together, just the two of you.

Now you reveal that yet another change is about to occur, that all those one-on-one trips to the mall, pizzas split down the middle, and homework done in tandem will soon be shared with someone else in your life. By announcing, no matter how gently, that you are involved with someone else, you have once again shaken your child's primary trust in you. You had told your daughter that you stopped loving her mommy, and that is why you divorced. But you also promised her that you would never stop loving her. Yet now you have revealed that not only do you have a life when you and she are not together, but also that you have found someone else to love. That person has now become so important to you that you are going to end the bilateral relationship you and your child have had since your divorce and change it to a triangle of child, co-parent, and significant other. Understand that your child will justifiably feel that you have been cheating on her with someone else, someone whom you now expect her to meet, like, and welcome into her life.

This situation is really rough on your child. At first, he will act as

6: INTRODUCING NEW PEOPLE INTO YOUR CHILD'S LIFE

if he likes your new boyfriend or girlfriend. You will beam with self-satisfaction, content that you can so smoothly integrate your new relationship into your life with your child. But your child has become a good actor; he is just putting on a face to please the parent he loves. In reality, he is not only still dealing with the losses of the divorce but also now with the collapse of his fantasy for parental reunification. Your child will smile. He will be nice, at least at first. But know that inside he may be seething with anger, frustrated at his lack of control. He may also be frightened and repulsed by the whole idea of your being in a relationship.

When you finally do embark on a new serious relationship that you feel is real and that will be in your life for a long time to come, then that is the time to introduce the new person to your children. But you must tell your ex first. Understand: you are not asking your ex for permission or for consent. You are merely informing her, as your custody agreement mandates, that a significant event in the life of the child you two created is about to occur. You do not want to blindside your ex or to have him hear from the kids "Guess who we met today?" Your ex, your partner in the co-parenting business, needs to know that a change to the business plan is on the horizon. You are about to bring in an associate. Of course, you and your ex remain the co-parents, but this new associate will be around for some time and will certainly end up playing a role in the life of your child. The new friend is not a co-parent, but as long as she is part of your life, she will be part of your child's life and a part of your ex's life, too, so the other co-parent needs to be made aware first, before you tell your child.

So you ask, "How do I do that?" You just convey the facts: "I have been dating someone for nine months. Her name is . . . She works at . . . She too is divorced and has a daughter a bit older than our son. This weekend I am going to tell our son about my new friend. Next week he and I are going to have lunch with her. Then he and I will be meeting her daughter. After that, some of the time that I am with our son, I will also be with my new friend and her daughter. Of course, I love our son deeply, and will be on the lookout for his emotions and reactions. I know this new situation can be complicated for him and that he might put on a good face for me but tell you how much this makes him unhappy. If he does, please let me know. I hope both of us can help him adjust to this new reality in our lives."

When it comes to introducing your child to your new relationship, it must be done slowly and in stages. (It is also advisable that your new friend not be visibly pregnant when she and your child meet.) Even though you first told your ex, your child's co-parent, about your new relationship, that co-parent must not be the one to inform the child. She may think she can better soften the blow than you. Or perhaps she is the one with the new lover, and you see the news as ammunition, which will let you prove yet again to your daughter that her mother is unreliable. Perhaps you are outraged because the lover your ex plans to introduce to your child is the reason your marriage broke up. No matter the situation, the co-parent with the new lover is the one who breaks the news to the child.

You will need to plot out very carefully the actual time and location of where and when to introduce your children to this new reality and to your new friend. First, this must be done in person; not on the phone, not via email, not in a YouTube video, and not in a text. Talk to your child while she is at your home. Not only should your new companion not be there for this conversation, but he is also not to show up afterward. If you alternate weekends with your ex, tell your child one weekend, and then wait until the next time she stays with you before introducing her to your new friend. The wait may be tedious for you and your lover, who wants to move forward in your relationship and who understands the role meeting your child plays in that, but it is essential to allow the child time to process the news and to ask both co-parents questions.

When the time comes, a week or two later, for your child to meet your new friend, pick a neutral setting: a park or a playground for a younger child, a restaurant for lunch with an older child. Do not pick a family holiday, birthday celebration, or any structured event for this first meeting. Your child will need the freedom to react and to question. He may be thrilled, angry, depressed, withdrawn, cautious, or even all of the above. This first meeting should be relatively brief: the hour or two it takes to play in the park or order and eat lunch. Let your child discover your friend for himself. Note: Your child's radar antenna will be on full alert. You will be transmitting the wrong message if you play footsies under the table or steal a kiss while your child climbs up the slide.

Most important, make no comparisons to your ex. This is not the time to discuss your child's other co-parent. Instead, this is a moment for two important people in your life to meet. You and your lover must answer questions honestly, telling the truth, but not divulging unnecessary details. Most children need not know that you are sleeping with your new friend on alternate weekends.

Resist the urge to make a threesome out of your next custodial weekend. Even though your child has learned, as children of divorce do, to tell you what you want to hear, and even though she says she would love spending the weekend with your new friend, your child approaches sharing you with trepidation. One way to reassure her, to let her know that she remains primary in your life, is for the two of you to spend your next weekend together as you have been doing since your separation: no third wheel wanted. Gradually lengthen the time and intensity of contact your child has with your new friend. Alternate times of threesomes with times of twosomes. If your new partner also has children, introduce them little by little to yours. However, just as you have never chosen your child's friends in the past, you cannot possibly demand that your child become friends with your lover's kids.

When your child is with you, do not have sleepovers with your new friend. Many divorce agreements prohibit members of the opposite sex unrelated by blood or marriage from sleeping over when the children are in the home. If that is the case, sleepovers may lead you into litigation. But even if your agreement permits such activities, and even if Freud was wrong about the irrevocable damage to the child who witnessed her parents making love (Freud's primal scene), nevertheless most children do not want to be confronted with parental sexuality. Also consider your child's—and your ex's—religious and moral standards. Neither your ex nor your child have veto power over your adult decisions, but you do not want your adult decisions to undermine or hurt your child.

When, despite the best intentions, indiscretions occur—your friend is having dinner with you and the kids, and it begins to snow; or you and your friend went to a party, and he had a little too much to drink, so he cannot drive home—do not flaunt your sleeping with your friend in front of your kids. Respect your child's emotions; understand how troubled she may be by seeing you sleep with someone else in front of her. Frankly, it is best at first for your new friend to sleep in the guest room. Obviously, over time, this will not be realistic, but the idea all along is to give your child time to get used to the change. Also do not let your friend walk around the house in boxers or in a Victoria's Secret nightie. Don't grope each other during breakfast. Just as you gradually introduced your child to your friend, gradually let the child see how this new relationship is intensifying and developing.

As the other co-parent, you will hear one day from your child that

Mom's new friend had a sleepover. Do not overreact. Don't expect your ex to have confided plans to take this step or to have asked your permission. If your divorce agreement prohibited unrelated people sleeping over, then address that as you would any other issue or challenge to the legal agreement, and it is certainly fair to raise with your ex your concerns about how this will impact your child.

A Stepparent Is Not a Co-Parent

Janet and Greg divorced nine years ago. They shared legal custody for their two sons, twelve-year-old Steven and ten-year-old Alex, with the boys living about two-thirds of the time with Janet and one-third with Greg. After the first year of skirmishes, there had been only relatively minor legal interventions, but a pervasive air of mistrust remained. Greg remarried several years after his divorce and became the stepparent of a seven-year-old girl. He and Elaine, his second wife, also had a daughter, now aged five. Janet had not remarried.

The relationship between the adults, cordial at first, had grown increasingly strained. Seemingly small issues became important ones. Elaine had become a vegetarian; she bought organic foods and hormone-free milk, and had become active in PETA (People for the Ethical Treatment of Animals) and in her neighborhood food co-op.

Her newfound passions influenced Greg's sons. The boys asked Janet if the food she cooked was organic. Steven stopped eating meat, saying he did not want to kill animals. Alex soon did the same. Both told Janet to buy organic produce. Janet wished she could, but, as a single parent on a tight, fixed income, she could not afford to do so. She also did not think growing boys should be vegetarians. She thought their health required that they eat meat and chicken.

One morning Janet and Greg met at a Starbucks, as they often did when email exchanges failed to bring agreement. As Greg explained

Elaine's vegetarian position, he failed to notice Janet's comments becoming curter and curter, her willingness to discuss fading. As in their other meetings, Greg had not understood that, while Janet recognized Greg's point of view in making decisions about Steven and Alex, she had absolutely no interest in what Elaine thought was best for her boys. The more Greg tried to explain Elaine's point of view, the more Janet shut down. When it came to raising her children, Janet allowed Elaine no influence.

Face-to-face co-parenting discussions require only two people: the two co-parents. Each parent has his or her own prescription for parenting. Your new spouse will surely add to the arsenal of parenting styles, tips, and tricks you have learned from your own parents and friends and from reading about how to raise your child. However, your child's stepparent does not have a place in this discussion. If you want to incorporate what the stepparent thinks and says, then bring those ideas to the coffee bar as part of your attitudes and beliefs. If Greg had said, "I want the children to eat organic as much as possible," Janet might have accepted his position. When he said that Elaine thought it better for them to eat organic, Janet shut down. Not only did she have absolutely no interest in raising her child according to Elaine's dictates, but she also legally had no obligation to consider Elaine's position.

Of course, Janet would have known that Greg, who, when they were married, ate as often as possible at McDonald's, had changed his views because of Elaine. But their conversation would have proceeded far more productively if it were Greg who wanted the children to eat organic and not Elaine. While Janet would well have understood Elaine's influence on Greg, the critical issue would have been that wanting his boys to eat organic produce was his desire, not Elaine's. Janet would have known that she had no right to interfere with Greg's convictions, any more than Greg would have the right to impose his new views on food on her.

As part of the dictate "Speak no evil about your ex to your children," each parent is obligated to support the positions of the other parent as long as their behaviors do not contradict pediatrician's recommendations, teachers' reports, or the law. For your children to be emotionally healthy, you must support your ex's positions. Greg should tell his sons: "Elaine and I believe that organic vegetables and fruits are better, but not everyone agrees with us. Organic foods are more expensive. When we can, we buy them. But there is nothing wrong with eating non-organic foods. It is more important to eat a healthy diet of plenty of fruits and vegetables. They do not have to be organic. Your mom does not have to buy organic produce just because we do in our house."

Supporting your ex's decisions is a far more potent indicator of your child's future success in life than whether he eats organic produce some of the time or all of the time. Instead of telling your child, "I feel strongly about this," it is better to say, "Your mom and I may have different ways of doing things, and you will follow both. Both are okay." Co-parenting, especially with stepparents, means recognizing that your child will grow up in households with different values and practices.

You know that good co-parenting also means involving the child and your ex in meaningful aspects of your life and considering how your choices and decisions will impact your child. So when you decide to become engaged and plan to marry, both your child and your ex have a right to know. Do not do what I know others have done: It's your weekend to have the children. You pack them into the car with your new friend on your way out to a special dinner. Before you get there, you stop and get married.

Bringing a stepparent into the co-parenting relationship complicates the family in other ways that are more unpredictable and less easy to resolve. A stepparent might be a caring adult and a fine influence for your child. Or a stepparent can be Cinderella's wicked stepmother, and you keep wishing that a fairy godmother would make her disappear. If you and your former spouse have accepted the divorce, moved on with your lives, and entered healthy new relationships, your remarriage can bring into your family an important new adult to enrich your child's life. But when anger persists or erupts—because the stepparent was the reason the marriage ended; because the stepparent tries to become a third parent; because the stepparent is closer in age to your child than to your ex; because your ex has turned co-parenting responsibilities over to the stepparent; or because of financial bitterness and jealousy—you've got troubles.

As you divorced, you and your ex developed arrangements for your child—who picked him up from soccer on weekdays, which weekends each month she stayed with Mom. But now someone new, who may also be divorced, who may also have children and co-parenting responsibilities, has entered your ex's life. Now you have been asked to accommodate this person's schedule.

All of a sudden, you find yourself juggling two sets of visitation and living arrangements. Your ex always has your child the same weekend his new spouse has hers. He asks to switch weekends with you, but that complicates your plans and impacts your child, who has fallen into her own routine. Your kids know, after all the arguments and legal battles, how difficult it is to switch custodial times.

It's enough to make you wonder why you ever thought that remarrying was worth the hassle. But if you remember to respect the precepts of your co-parenting relationship, keep your eye on the welfare of your child, and respect some important boundaries, you can do this.

6: INTRODUCING NEW PEOPLE INTO YOUR CHILD'S LIFE

And you can wind up with even greater benefits for your child in the long run.

The ideal stepparent plays an extensive and meaningful role in the life of your child. She is now there every day when the child is in your ex's home. If she is the cook, your child eats her meals. If he does the basketball practice pickup, your child spends time alone in the car with him.

Stepparents, even those who played a painful role in the dissolution of your marriage, are going to influence your child. Their values, mannerisms, habits, disciplinary styles, language, and expectations all now become part of the home where your child lives part of the time. How much impact stepparents have varies greatly. Psychologists understand the complex, interactive influence of all environmental inputs on the personality, behaviors, and decision-making processes of children. Stepparents certainly have an effect, but so too do the twenty hours a week your child spends with electronics (phone, computer, games, TV), the fabulous fourth-grade teacher she has, his very best friend, and the queen bee of the group with her lunch mates. Your child's individual growth and development is influenced by all these factors. The introduction of one more influence, the stepparent, while certainly important, is not, in and of itself, decisive.

The day-to-day tasks of the new stepparent will depend largely on the age of the child. Stepparenting a sixteen-year-old who drives and who has a voice in where she lives means supervision and discussion, not childcare. Stepparenting a toddler coming out of diapers is an entirely different thing.

But remember: Stepparents are not co-parents. They are involved in the daily life of your child, but they do not meet with your ex to negotiate, plan, and strategize for your child. Your ex remains your child's only other co-parent.

Make sure the new spouse doesn't try to take over the parenting role of your former spouse. He can play a supporting part to you as the child's parent and take on minor responsibilities that don't undermine your ex's role. For instance it's the co-parents who set up the pediatrician visit and decide on the tutor, while the stepparent may give the prescribed medicine in the morning and do some of the driving to the tutor. If the stepparent wants to discuss parenting decisions, it should be done behind the scenes with her partner and presented as the co-parent's idea.

Meanwhile, the stepparent should work hard to respect the role of his spouse's ex and support the love the child has for his other parent, taking care not to undermine it. If Dad is the baseball coach, don't volunteer to run the baseball tournament. Teach your stepchild how to fish instead. If Mom volunteers in school, don't step on her toes and offer to be on the parent-teacher association. Teach your stepchild how to cook instead.

Early in the relationship, stepparents should also avoid being the primary disciplinarians. Few things upset a parent more than a stepparent physically disciplining a child. There are other effective ways of promoting safety and enforcing guidelines. Stepparents may use alternatives to physical discipline in a way that is acceptable to both parents. They can model positive behaviors, treat the stepchild respectfully, and reward them for appropriate actions. They may react to safety issues, but let the biological parent deal with major problems. As the stepparenting relationship evolves over time, the stepparent can join with his or her partner to establish new family guidelines and rules.

Of course, if you are the other co-parent, you must ultimately accept that your ex is now raising your child with a new partner. You may despise the paths they take together, but you should not denigrate them in front of your child. You wield power and influence in raising your child, not by demeaning your ex and his new partner, but by teaching your child your core values, beliefs, and expectations. If the values and beliefs of your ex and new partner are at odds with yours, your child will observe both and over time accept the pattern of behavior appropriate for her.

If you are the parent bringing in a stepparent to the dynamic, you should discuss with your ex and with your new partner what the stepparent's role will be and how it must suit the needs of the new family system. Go slowly; the stepparent's relationship with the child will evolve over time. Your child probably won't love him or her the first few months of this new relationship, and the stepparent probably won't love the child right away, either. Don't rush it; relationships take time.

CHAPTER 7

Accusations of Abuse or Abusive Accusations?

Bob and Fran had been married for thirteen years when they decided to divorce. Five years earlier, while they were trying to get pregnant with their daughter, Sophia, Bob had an affair with a colleague. And though Fran had decided to reconcile and stay together for the sake of their child, the marriage never truly recovered; Fran sought out a divorce attorney.

But she was unprepared for the havoc divorce would wreak in her life, her husband's life, and especially her child's life when the attorney began looking for ways to give her a financial edge in the divorce settlement—whether justified or not.

She had not previously considered the financial ramifications of the costs of retaining a lawyer and of litigating the custody fight. She was just beginning to understand that she would likely lose her house and that divorce meant not only losing her spouse but also a radical change in her lifestyle. Rather than face all this, she again urged Bob into counseling. But by the time they began working with a new therapist, Fran recognized that the marriage was indeed over.

The next time she met with her lawyer, she asked if there were any circumstances that would lessen the financial impact of divorce and allow her and Sophia to remain in the marital home. Her attorney indicated that judges preferred an equal distribution of financial resources except in cases of abuse. The attorney then began to grill Fran: Had there been any abuse in the marriage? Fran recalled Bob raising his voice during arguments, but he had never threatened or struck her. What about his relationship with Sophia? Fran could not recall times when Bob had either neglected or hurt his child. Then she said that, in fact, the opposite was true: Bob had a very intense and emotional relationship with this child; he loved her.

The attorney pounced on Fran for details. What did she mean by emotionally intense? How did he love his daughter? Fran recalled a Saturday morning where Bob ran errands with Sophia. He had insisted on taking her on one more errand. When they returned, about a half hour later, Fran described that Sophia was exhausted and had a look that was not her own. Fran had asked Sophia whether anyone had bothered her, and the five-year-old had said no. Then Fran had asked if anyone had ever hurt her, and Laurie said a ghost had hurt her. Fran thought she was just dealing with a five-year-old's imagination. The lawyer was not so sure. Their meeting ended, and she asked Fran to think, before they next met, if she could remember other occasions when Sophia seemed odd after having been with her father.

That afternoon Fran began asking Sophia more about the incident. Sophia now said that she had not been hurt. Then Fran asked her five-year-old whether anyone had ever touched her "down there." Laurie said the ghost did; but she displayed no discomfort or distress as she said this. Fran then asked Sophia who was the ghost. Sophia lightly said: "Daddy's the ghost."

7: ACCUSATIONS OF ABUSE OR ABUSIVE ACCUSATIONS?

A week later Fran returned to her attorney and relayed her conversation with Sophia. The attorney raised the possibility that Bob was sexually abusing his daughter. Fran was shocked. She did not believe that Bob would touch their daughter sexually. However, the lawyer persisted asking questions based on a range of reactions associated with child sexual abuse. Did Sophia ever seem excessively tired? Did she periodically cling to one parent? Had she ever had trouble sleeping at night? Did she, at times, seem to withdraw into her own world? Answering yes to these questions may be considered markers of child sexual abuse, but frankly, what five-year-old does not sometimes cling to Mommy when tired or wake up in the middle of the night? Not all children with these behaviors are abused. Not surprisingly, Fran answered yes to most questions. The attorney then said that she was concerned that Bob had sexually abused Sophia and that the child must immediately be evaluated by a therapist. She gave Fran the name of one she had worked with on similar cases in the past.

The next day Fran met the "counselor," a young therapist of indeterminate qualifications who had indeed worked with this attorney but who had very limited experience dealing with suspected child sexual abuse. Fran related that she feared her daughter had been sexually abused by her husband and explained the incident following the trip and Sophia's responses about the ghost and Daddy. The therapist asked to see Sophia that afternoon for an evaluation.

During the evaluation, Sophia, with a child's vivid imagination, described in detail how ghosts attacked her, how snakes crawled on her, and how she didn't like to play alone. When the therapist asked her who was the ghost, the child replied, "My daddy's the ghost. That is what Mommy told me, and that is what I told Mommy." During the session the therapist asked Sophia to draw pictures. The counselor interpreted one of the scribbles as sexual. Still, the counselor remained unsure about how to handle the situation. She was not firmly convinced that Sophia had been sexually abused.

The next morning the attorney contacted the counselor for her report and reiterated her concern that Sophia had been sexually abused. The counselor replied that she was unsure and needed more time to evaluate. The attorney reminded the counselor that state law mandates that health care providers report immediately any suspicion of abuse to the county child protective services agency. It was the therapist's responsibility to make that report, not to determine whether or not abuse had occurred. Even as the counselor protested that she wasn't sure that she had suspicion of abuse, the attorney pressed her, claiming that the safety of the child was at stake and that she must protect the child. She could continue her evaluation process once the report was made. The counselor contacted Child Protective Services and followed up with a letter indicating that she believed the father had abused the child and asking that the agency not allow the father to have any unsupervised contact with his daughter.

Child Protective Services immediately intervened, issued a restraining order, and required Bob to move out of the house. Fran filed for divorce and charged her ex with abusing their daughter. For the child's welfare, the counselor now insisted on treating Sophia several times a week. Sophia, who had been a somewhat fragile child before all this, spent those sessions talking about ghosts and snakes and having her drawings and play interpreted as revealing long-standing sexual maltreatment. The counselor, Fran, and the Child Protective Services worker constantly focused Sophia on the identity of "the ghost." Laurie kept repeating: "I have already told you, Daddy's the ghost."

Bob immediately hired a team of lawyers and filed for custody of Sophia, claiming that Fran was slandering him and negatively influencing their child. Child Protective Services, based on the counselor's conviction that Sophia's play revealed sexual maltreatment, filed a finding of child sexual abuse and called for the police and prosecutor's office to pursue the case. However, without any physical evidence of sexual maltreatment, the prosecutor's office did not feel that it had the evidence it needed to file criminal charges.

Nevertheless, Bob was prohibited from having any contact with his daughter except under the supervision of a social worker. He and Sophia continued to meet once a week in the social worker's office, where their interactions were videotaped. Months of supervised visitation produced no evidence of inappropriate contacts or talk between Bob and his daughter. To the contrary, Sophia really looked forward to seeing her father each week, and she was quite appropriate in her interactions with him: neither sexualized, overly friendly, nor removed and distant. Even as Sophia's therapist continued to report the child's struggle with the aftermath of sexual maltreatment, Sophia's supervising social worker saw no evidence of any concern.

As the court date to determine custody drew near, Fran fired her original attorney. She hired a new lawyer and asked the court to extend the date of the hearing so that he could prepare. The court, with its customary backlog, readily agreed. Sophia's custody hearing was finally held a year and a half after the original accusation of abuse was reported to Child Protective Services. For the past year and a half, nearly a quarter of the child's six-and-a-half years, Sophia had seen her father only once a week in the social worker's office. While Bob had tried to maintain elements of normality during these meetings—bringing lunch for himself and Sophie, reading her stories that would continue from week to week—the relationship, lacking sufficient time together and ordinary settings, had become increasingly awkward. Sophia, who had so enjoyed seeing her father in their first meetings, was no longer close to him. Meeting him under supervision for a year and a half, much like a child visiting a parent in jail, had taken its toll. Their relationship was strained and restricted. Sophie did not know her father very well.

In the end, the court did not find that Sophia had been sexually abused. But a year and a half of being treated as such in her counselor's and social worker's offices had an impact. Sophia had become quite shy and withdrawn. She often refused to separate from her mother to go to school. She had become a finicky eater and socially isolated. Her parents had spent hours and hours preparing for trial and hundreds of thousands of dollars on expert witnesses and legal fees. What had begun as an attempt to gain the upper hand in a custody hearing had spun wildly out of control and made this fragile child into a pawn between her two parents.

Now, after the custody hearing, as contact was reestablished between Bob and Sophia, the damage had already been done. Although the court demanded the parents deal with each other in determining significant issues in the life of the child, essentially a form of co-parenting, they had no mechanisms in place to do that. What they had was a year and a half of accusations and venom and a damaged child who they would have to raise to maturity together.

It is imperative to understand the potential ramifications of accusations of maltreatment and abuse. These are powerful charges. If indeed a parent has physically abused a child, the child must be protected. But to raise a charge of abuse in order to try to get a better financial settlement is unconscionable. Even unfounded accusations of abuse stain the reputation of the accused, perhaps for a lifetime. Equally importantly, they have the potential to cause great harm to your child.

Unfortunately, accusations of abuse have become common in divorce proceedings. Spouses charge each other with physical and emotional abuse. One parent will claim the other physically and even sexually abused their child. Today's contentious divorces all too often include restraining orders. These may prohibit one spouse from coming within a hundred yards of the other; or they may prevent a parent from seeing the child; or they may permit visits, but only under supervision. In some towns and counties today, accusations of abuse are such a common part of divorce proceedings that reporting them has become a game of who runs first to the sheriff's office to file the restraining order.

Sometimes, however, accusations of abuse are fueled, not by parental fights, but by zealous lawyers eager to gain an upper hand in the proceedings. In these cases, what began as a legal maneuver can spin out of your control and cannot be stopped. In the end, it may ruin the lives of both your ex and your child.

It is important to understand that the police and other authorities usually do not fully investigate calls about domestic violence in divorcing couples. They are uninterested in causes and may not look for bruises and marks if they are not readily visible. Instead, they attempt to reinstate the peace. They do that by just telling the accused to "get out" of the house. The parent charging abuse goes to the courthouse and files to get a restraining order that will, at least legally and theoretically, keep the ex a hundred yards away from the parent or the child until a court hearing.

An emergency hearing on a restraining order can easily take a week or two to schedule. Meanwhile, your ex, the accused, has had to move out of the house if he or she was still living there. Also, all of a sudden your ex has no contact with your child. The restraining order paints your ex as guilty until proven innocent. Your friends and neighbors will think: "He must have beaten her up if he can't get back into the house." This new context colors their memories of other interactions: "He always had a violent temper. Remember how he screamed at the kids when they broke the swing?"

Your job is to protect your child. If you believe your child was physically or sexually abused, you must take action. Pick up the phone and call the police, Child Protective Services, or another local child welfare agency dedicated to protecting children. These agencies, found in every county, must investigate all cases where they suspect abuse or maltreatment.

Emotional abuse—when a parent deliberately tries to cause psychological and emotional harm to a child—is very difficult to assess and to prove because it leaves no bruises for you or anyone else to see. Not surprisingly, child welfare agencies often hesitate to investigate charges of emotional abuse, in part because it is so difficult to get evidence to prosecute these cases. Nevertheless, if you have serious concerns that your ex is emotionally abusing your child, report it.

Regardless of how much you hate your ex and how much better off you think your child would be if your ex were not around, do not suggest abuse is taking place if you know in your heart that it is not. The effects of such an act will negatively affect your child in ways that you cannot even imagine for years to come.

CHAPTER 8

When Your Ex Just Says No

Norman and Cynthia had a contentious marriage for a number of years. Norman had lost several jobs after he had harassed female staff, but with the charm of a natural-born salesman, he had always managed to land on his feet. However, the last time he was fired, charges were filed against him for sexual harassment and attempted rape of a female coworker. In a settlement the charges were reduced to a misdemeanor and the case file sealed.

Cynthia sued for divorce, but because the record was closed, Norman's sexual acting-out could not be used in the hearing. Norman's lawyer insisted on joint legal custody and joint physical custody, with five-year-old Simon living with his father half the time. Cynthia and her attorney were convinced that this was just a negotiating ploy and knew they were right when Norman offered to drop the joint physical custody in exchange for lower spousal support and joint legal custody. Cynthia agreed. She was certain that soon Norman would not be seeing Simon every other weekend as they had agreed, since his new girlfriend and new job were about a hundred miles away. She figured that he would quickly drop out of their lives.

Right after the divorce Norman did move, but now he insisted that Cynthia drive Simon a hundred miles each way every other weekend for visitation. The original custody decree had not considered this issue, because the exes then lived a few miles apart. When Cynthia refused to drive their son one weekend, Norman filed a contempt of court charge against her. They settled and agreed that Cynthia would drive Simon two-thirds of the distance each way, about sixty-five miles, and they would transfer him at a McDonald's off the highway. On Friday afternoons Cynthia could get there in an hour and a quarter, but the trip home, with rush-hour traffic, took more than two hours. On Sunday afternoons, she had to leave at least two and half hours before the exchange because traffic was unpredictable, and the one time she was delayed because of it, Norman ignored her phone calls and took Simon back to his house. Cynthia had had to drive all the way there to pick up her son.

Norman grew increasingly empowered by his success at manipulating Cynthia and interfered with Simon's life and Cynthia's decisions more and more. When Cynthia enrolled Simon in a full-day kindergarten program because she felt he was ready for it and so she could look for part-time work while Simon was in school, Norman protested. He invoked their agreement, which mandated that parents consult each other about important decisions affecting their child and insisted Simon should attend half-day kindergarten. He thought Simon was just too young to be in school all day and that he paid child and spousal support so that Cynthia could do her job and stay home to raise their son. Cynthia and Norman argued about the kindergarten the next time they exchanged Simon at the McDonald's. Two days later Norman sent a certified letter to the superintendent of schools (not copying Cynthia), enclosing his custody order and refusing permission for Simon to attend full-day kindergarten. With less than a week until the new school year began, the school board attorney advised the principal that unless both parents approved, Simon could not attend full-day kindergarten. Cynthia had no recourse. Even if she wanted to spend the money and take Norman to court, she would never get a hearing before that all-important first day of class.

Nominal courtesy between the exes ended; they communicated only through curt emails. Norman began demanding a detailed accounting of Simon's activities each day. Cynthia usually did not respond.

But six-year-old Simon responded to all the conflict quite acutely, showing signs of stress and anxiety. He crawled into his mother's bed at night. Teachers reported that he was tearful, sucked on his shirtsleeves, and twirled his hair. Simon was withdrawing from playdates and avoiding social settings. His pediatrician referred Simon to a child psychologist for evaluation.

Cynthia never told Norman. She went ahead and scheduled an interview for herself with the child psychologist. The psychologist asked to meet with Norman, but before that request was conveyed, Norman got an insurance form showing the charge for the psychological consultation. He fired off another letter, this time to the psychologist. He sent the court order and demanded the psychologist stop consulting with or treating his child. The psychologist, who had not yet met Simon, implored Norman to meet with him, but Norman refused. He said that his son did not need to see any psychologist, and that he, the legal joint custodial parent, had never been consulted about the matter.

Norman also wrote Simon's pediatrician. He demanded that he be informed in advance of any of Simon's appointments and wrote that the pediatrician could not diagnose, treat, or prescribe medication for Simon, except in life-threatening emergencies, without first consulting with and receiving approval from Norman. The pediatrician replied that Norman was invited to attend every doctor's visit and participate in the feedback and treatment plan, but that his schedule did not allow him time to call Norman about every visit and recommendation. When Norman replied that under the terms of his custody agreement, the pediatrician had to get his consent to treat Simon, the pediatrician bowed out of Simon's care, leaving Cynthia to find another doctor for her son. She hired a new attorney to file sanctions against Norman, whose behavior had become utterly out of control, and she charged that he had obstructed her decision making.

Meanwhile, one of the dads in Cynthia's neighborhood was organizing and coaching a kindergarten spring soccer team. All of Simon's friends were going to play. The league was instructional. The boys would not yet play games. They would practice during the week and learn soccer skills while getting to wear uniforms, and each would get a trophy at the end of the season. Simon was really excited and told his father about his new blue jersey and his coach. Once again Norman objected. He argued that since Simon was having difficulty adjusting to kindergarten—his mother knew this because she wanted to take him to a child psychologist—he could not possibly expose his son to the additional stress of soccer right now.

Besides, Norman argued, he planned to register Simon next fall in the soccer league in his city. It played weekend games. He told Cynthia that Simon should abandon his team and that Cynthia should bring him on her custodial weekends to the games in Norman's town. Norman, who had never played sports, also declared he planned to help coach the team so that Simon could fully benefit and "enhance the quality of his social experiences under appropriate parental supervision."

Simon's soccer coach hit the roof. He called Norman an idiot and told him that Simon was going to play with his friends on this team. He told Norman that, unless a judge instructed him otherwise, he was not bound by anything Norman said or wrote. He also told Norman to grow up and stop destroying his ex's and his child's life.

Norman threatened injunctions and court orders to compel Cynthia to cease making decisions without his consent. This time, thanks to the support and encouragement of the neighborhood coach, Cynthia told Norman to shove it. She told him to go ahead and file with the court to stop Simon from playing soccer.

Norman set out to do that, but he discovered that he had to file in the county where the divorce had taken place. His former attorney, surely exasperated by Norman's obstructionist behavior, quoted him an exorbitant fee to take on the case. Norman called other attorneys; none would file to prevent Simon from playing in a kindergarten soccer league. Cynthia, seeing herself triumphant for the first time over her bullying ex, mustered up the courage to tell her attorney to change her filing in court to request a change of custody. They ended up in my office after their new agreement ordered parent coordination. Legal custody never changed, but now, with a court-ordered psychologist and parent coordinator looking over his shoulder, Norman has backed off from his bullying.

When your lawyer and friends persuaded you to give your ex joint legal custody, you thought it really wouldn't matter much. While you were married, your ex could not even name your child's piano teacher; he didn't even remember how to drive to your child's best friend's house. As co-parent, you thought your ex surely wouldn't get involved in the day-to-day life of your child. He just wanted to be named co-parent to save face. He did not want his parents, siblings, friends, and coworkers thinking that he lost, that you got sole legal custody. You knew you and your ex would fight over some matters—especially expensive items that you knew your child needed. But you figured all the financial issues would be worked out in the final divorce decree. You figured you could handle your ex on the other stuff. In the past you always made all the decisions. You chose the pediatrician; you chose your child's after-school activities; you arranged the playdates. Why should that change now?

You figured that once your ex was named co-parent, he would be like all those other divorced dads you knew, minimally involved in their kids' lives. He would see your child occasionally. They would go to the movies and to sporting events, but otherwise your ex would be what he has always been, self-absorbed. His work and new social life would fill his days and take him out of your life and that of your child.

But you discovered soon after the final decree that you were dead wrong. Your joint legal custody is changing your life and that of your child in ways you never anticipated.

Unfortunately, joint legal custody affords the potential for one parent to bully the other. Effective joint legal custody requires compromise, consensus, or consent for major decisions affecting the child. When one parent just says no, he hampers the ability to raise the child. If that parent routinely says no—no to the pediatrician, no to the psychologist, no to the tutor, no to the soccer team, no to piano lessons, no to gymnastics—that parent inhibits the other from effectively raising the child. Threatening doctors, teachers, and coaches keeps most of them at bay. They do not want to get involved; they fear legal consequences. They stand back, and you are left feeling alone and helpless.

Meanwhile your ex has discovered websites promoting fathers' rights, and he disingenuously uses the ideas posted there to frustrate and block your plans for your child.

First, he blocks you where you knew he would, in matters related to money. You know your daughter should have braces. But your ex calls your child's dentist, who concedes that braces are not a "medical necessity," a term used in your divorce decree that you had never thought much about, so your ex refuses to pay even for the orthodontist consultation. You want your daughter to have straight teeth, so you weigh your options. Your attorney thinks you will likely win in court to get him to share the cost of the braces, but a hearing will probably cost as much as the braces themselves. So you either back down and put off the braces for this year, hoping that, as your daughter matures, your ex will see that she indeed needs a perfect smile, or you bite the bullet and pay for them yourself.

Either way, your ex has grown even bossier after winning this round of the battle. He realizes he can just say no, and there is little you can do about it.

Your Ex Is a Bully

What can you do? Simon's soccer coach knew that the best way to deal with a bully is to call his bluff. You need to do the same. The next time a problem arises, inform your ex of his choices. Do not get frustrated and drawn into an argument. Instead document, for yourself and potentially for a future court action, your ex's unreasonableness and refusal to compromise. When you want to get your son tested for allergies because he keeps getting hay fever and your ex claims children get allergies from allergy testing, you counter that the American Academy of Pediatricians recommends this for children with your son's symptoms and that your pediatrician agrees. When your ex still refuses consent, go ahead and make the rational decision for your child. You can, if you wish, file emergency court motions on each issue as it arises, or you can wait for your ex to try to block you or charge you with contempt after the fact.

If your ex threatens to take you to court charging contempt when you are following your pediatrician's advice or the advice of your son's teacher who says he is ready for a full-day kindergarten or should see a psychologist because of the stress incurred by the divorce or for any reason, let your ex go ahead and do that. The judges I have worked with will not be sympathetic. You will need to show the court, if the matter gets that far, your emails indicating that you informed your ex about the allergy testing or school plan and attempted to discuss the issues with him. This time, when your ex takes you to court, you countersue for your legal fees and court costs and ask also that your ex be enjoined from blocking your appropriate parental decision making. The first time you appear before a judge for this kind of matter, your ex will likely be told to be more accommodating in the future. But if he takes you back to court on similar matters in the future, he may eventually end up paying your court costs and legal fees.

In intractable situations like that of Norman and Cynthia, the court may also decide to order parent coordination. The court may also set limits to joint legal custody, specifying which matters do not require the consent of both custodial legal parents. Once your obstructionist ex loses in court a few times, he will have learned that joint legal custody no longer works for venting his anger at you.

But whether you take your bully ex back to court, wait for him to take you back to court, or get help from school professionals or your doctor, do not bring your child into the conflict.

When your child asks, "Can I play soccer?" tell her that you and her dad are still working this one out. Don't tell her, "Your dad is a bullying son of a bitch." Your child is your daughter, not your friend.

Your ex may be a bully, but you'd better be sure you are not one, too. Check out your perspective with friends and family. A bully refuses his child essential medical care. But insisting for financial reasons that your daughter's doctor accept his health insurance does not make your ex a bully. A bully won't hire a tutor even when your child's teachers and school psychologist say it's the only way to raise her grades from

8: WHEN YOUR EX JUST SAYS NO

failing. Yet when your ex refuses to pay her half of a summer academic enrichment program in Spain that might look good on your son's college application, she is not a bully. The bully is adamant: His child will not participate in extracurricular activities. But just because he refuses to commit to weekends of driving out of state for hockey tournaments does not make your ex a bully.

No matter how affected your children are by your ex's intractable behavior, they are even more traumatized when you allow the situation to escalate the conflict and acrimony that they must endure. Your child is not being bullied; you are. Don't introduce your child into the conflict with your ex.

CHAPTER 9

The Ex with Psychological Problems

Mary and William had been divorced for more than a year when Mary walked into my office. They had had two children: a son, sixteen, and a daughter, thirteen. Her son no longer had any contact with her, and the parent's co-parenting arrangement was collapsing.

Mary had not worked outside her home since early in her marriage. But the divorce decree specified that she prepare to return to the workforce. It gave her two years of spousal support during which she would either finish college or pursue a training program. After that, spousal support would be phased out. During those two years Mary and the children would live in what had been the family home. But after the time was up, and once her daughter was ready for high school and her son was old enough to drive himself and his sister to school from either his father's condo or his mother's future residence, the house was to be sold. The future transition was designed to be sensitive to the needs of all parties—Mary would get the education she needed to get a job; the children would stay in their school; William would recoup his investment in the family home.

The only problem was that a year and a half after the divorce, the parties were stuck, and the transition to new living arrangements was nowhere on the horizon. I was brought into the case as a parent coordinator.

Mary sauntered into my office with a gift for me, a book on borderline personality disorders. Mary announced that she had divorced her husband because he had a borderline personality disorder, and she could no longer tolerate his unpredictable moods. People who suffer from the chronic psychological problem of borderline personality disorder exhibit unstable and turbulent emotions. Their attachments to individuals swing back and forth. One day the borderline person loves you, the next he hates you; there is no middle ground. Not surprisingly then, borderline individuals have trouble with relationships and on the job.

She claimed that she had forced William into treatment and had insisted that he begin mood-stabilizing medication. But when William saw no improvement after several months of psychotherapy and psychopharmacological drugs, he got a second opinion that did not corroborate his initial diagnosis. While William continued in therapy, primarily to discuss divorce options, he stopped taking his medications. She attributed the rage he now directed at her to his illness running amok.

Shortly after Mary and William separated, she became concerned that their son, John, not only also had a borderline personality disorder, but that he was bipolar. Bipolar disorder is a significant psychological mood disorder characterized by rapid, uncontrollable, and unpredictable mood swings. People with bipolar disorder have periods of depression, when they are lethargic and feel hopeless and helpless. They then rapidly shift into a period of mania, when they have so much energy that they need little sleep; their libidos go into overdrive; and they may have delusions of grandeur and act recklessly on them.

Mary took John to a number of psychologists and psychiatrists,

9: THE EX WITH PSYCHOLOGICAL PROBLEMS

but she complained to me that all were incompetent. They did not see the borderline and bipolar disorders; instead they kept saying John was reacting to the stress of the divorce. Mary knew better. She insisted that John undergo several comprehensive psychological, psychiatric, and neurological evaluations. By the time he got to his fourth evaluation with a psychiatrist, he was so angry that he refused to get out of the car. Mary managed to bribe and coax him into the evaluation, but he was hostile and verbally abusive. When the psychiatrist asked him the same mental status questions he had already answered no to several times—"Do you ever hear noises and voices in your head that are not really there? If you had three magic wishes, what would they be?"—John flipped out and began ranting about how much he hated his mother and how he sometimes wanted to kill her.

After this one brief meeting, this psychiatrist concurred with Mary: John indeed had both bipolar and borderline personality disorders that he had likely inherited from his father, whom the psychiatrist had never met and whose medical records he did not request. The psychiatrist prescribed a kitchen sink of medications to manage John's mental health.

Mary and John fought daily over his taking these medications. These fights proved to Mary that John was impulsive, reckless, and aggressive. Hence he could not possibly be trusted to drive a car. She refused to take him for his provisional driving test or to allow him to enroll in a driver's education class. John's hostility reaffirmed for Mary his dysfunctional psychological state.

John also displayed hostility toward his father, but mostly he saw William as weak and blamed his father for leaving him with Mary for so much of the time. One Sunday night, when the time came for John to return to his mother's home, he would not budge. Mary wanted her attorney to file contempt charges against William for letting John stay with him, but, given John's age, the attorney refused. Instead, the psychiatrist told Mary to wait. Sooner or later John's borderline personality disorder would manifest itself in shifting attachments. John would hate his father and return eagerly to the mother he loved. However, months had gone by, and John's "borderline personality disorder" had not yet kicked in to swing his affections toward his mother. By the time Mary came into my office, John had had nothing to do with her for many months.

Now Mary was deeply concerned about her daughter, Rachel. Mary saw her exhibiting a similar pattern of borderline personality disorder. Rachel had had a series of violent outbursts at home. She had thrown her calculator against a window and shoved a bunch of dishes to the floor. Formerly a good student, Rachel was now doing poorly in school. Mary insisted Rachel needed to be tested for learning disabilities, attention-deficit disorder, and language processing deficiencies. Mary then showed me her calendar: In the fourteen days before she and I first met, Mary had taken her daughter to two psychiatric counseling sessions, a psychoeducational evaluation, two speech and language assessments, her pediatrician (for sleeping problems), and a meeting at school to assess Rachel's learning disabilities. Rachel had also had a full blood workup. Mary mentioned that William, whose borderline personality disorder she made sure to explain to each of the experts she saw, had nominally participated in only one of these meetings: the one at school, where he pointed out that Rachel had had no record of academic or behavioral difficulties before the divorce.

During our meeting, Mary said she had to leave early because Rachel had stayed home from school that day with a cold, and Mary had to get home to take care of her. Mary later admitted that Rachel might not really have a cold. She thought Rachel might have stayed in bed because of anxiety over her problems and her trepidation about

9: THE EX WITH PSYCHOLOGICAL PROBLEMS

spending the coming weekend with her father and brother. But she also pointed out that Rachel had frequent viruses and gastrointestinal problems that her physicians had difficulty diagnosing and managing. Mary kept directing our discussion to Rachel's illnesses, even though she had come to my office because of the problems she was having co-parenting and moving forward to the next stage of the divorce plan.

It quickly became clear to me that Mary was in denial about the implications of her divorce. She had been repeatedly warned that spousal support would shortly end, but she had made no plans for training or education or finding a job. She was supposed to have arranged for repairs to the marital residence so that the house could go on the market, but she had not dealt with those either. She would not let William into the house to see what still needed to be fixed. When he sent over workmen to get estimates, Mary told them that her daughter had a highly contagious viral infection and that they had best not come in.

Rachel's suddenly emergent emotional and behavioral issues made it extremely difficult for Mary to go out to work. Who would take Rachel to psychotherapy, speech therapy, pediatrician visits, and school meetings, and stay home with her when she was ill, if not her mother? Mary did see herself as complying with the spirit of the plan. She had indeed applied for jobs, but each time she did, she described her daughter's schedule of psychotherapy, speech therapy, and tutoring, and explained how she must have a very flexible schedule to care for Rachel and take her to all her appointments. Not surprisingly, no one would hire Mary.

Mary assumed that because of these complications, the planned shift in living arrangements could not possibly take place. Because of William's and John's borderline personality disorders, how could Rachel, who was so fragile, be expected to live with them, even part of the time? Moreover, John had never gotten his license, and he would not be able to drive Rachel to high school, which was part of the original agreement. Furthermore, if Mary and Rachel would have to leave the marital home, that would further distress Rachel. Mary assumed that Rachel's psychological problems would trump the agreement from two years ago, and that she and Rachel would stay in their home.

The court, bewildered by lists of doctors and diagnoses for both children and William, ordered the couple into co-parent counseling, and that's where I came in. Mary smiled innocently as William explained that she had to get a job and move out of the house that they were going to sell. Mary replied by emphasizing William's anger. She had confided in Rachel: "Daddy wants to move you away from your house and school, wants me to get a job with long hours so you will be home alone, and is not going to buy our groceries anymore." Hearing this, Rachel became extremely upset, increasingly angry with her father, and more withdrawn and fragile. Her behavior only reinforced her mother's diagnosis of borderline personality disorder.

When Mary was confronted with concerns about her behaviors and told that not only would her marital home soon be sold but also that, as per the original agreement, spousal support would end, she turned on me, the parent counselor. Not until Rachel's therapist became convinced that Rachel's disorders were likely caused by Mary did Mary begin to give in.

Ultimately, the marital house was sold, but, because it was sold "as is," William and Mary lost tens of thousands of dollars in profit. Mary moved into the bedroom of a relative who lived nearby and took short-term jobs far below her qualifications. Although it took much persuading, Rachel began spending half her time with her father. Gradually she spent less and less time with her mother. Four years after the divorce, she was still fragile, but she was functioning academically and socially in a school near her father's house. On the other hand, John had dropped out of high school. After a series of low-level jobs, he had enlisted in the US armed forces and was training for combat.

It's Your Ex's Problem, Not Your Child's

Mary is an extreme example of someone suffering from undiagnosed and unchecked psychological issues that were not only preventing her from moving on with her life following divorce but were also causing very real damage to the psychological and physiological health of her children. Facing dramatic changes in her life that would cost her her home and force her to enter the workforce, she created illness within her family, believing that if her children were ill, she would have to care for them and would not be expected to move on.

In truth, Mary was ill with Munchausen Syndrome by Proxy, an emotional disorder in which a parent, because of her own needs, creates an illness in a healthy child. Munchausen Syndrome by Proxy, which is considered a form of child abuse, usually involves a parent inducing real or apparent symptoms of a disease in a child. The parent seems deeply devoted to the child. She takes him from specialist to specialist, from diagnostic procedure to diagnostic procedure, all in an attempt to get her child well again. But, in fact, she has created the illness, sometimes by giving the child drugs to simulate symptoms, other times by falsifying lab work or through emotional manipulation.

Divorce forces radical, perhaps unexpected, changes to your life and incurs an enormous amount of stress. It's a blow to your ego, to your self-esteem, and your sense of security and identity. You are overloaded and stressed, but at the same time, you may feel unwanted, unneeded, and suddenly lonely. This can be a great load to bear for anyone; for some it can lead to unforeseen and unexpected psychological problems.

A few parents ease their loneliness as Mary did, by making their children need them and depend on them more than ever before. If your child is ill, then your child cannot possibly get along without you. Especially in situations where the divorce compels a stay-at-home parent to return, after many years, to the workforce, the temptation to make certain your child will continue to "need me" may lead in problematic directions. This is a very real psychological condition that can frequently arise out of the stress of divorce.

But Munchausen Syndrome by Proxy is certainly not the only kind of psychological ailment that might threaten the co-parenting situation and the health of your child.

Fit to Parent?

Even in elementary school, Charlotte was tagged as "different." In third grade, diagnosed with learning disabilities and attention-deficit disorder, she was placed in a special education class. In high school she experimented with alcohol, drugs, and boys. By the time she was sixteen, she had been in and out of multiple therapists' offices and already had a police record for relatively minor behavior issues. But psychological testing revealed serious problems. Charlotte admitted that sometimes she heard voices telling her to do bad things. At other times her mind raced as a rush of ideas pushed and pulled her in different directions. A psychiatrist diagnosed schizophrenia and treated it pharmacologically, and Charlotte connected with a good psychologist. Charlotte stabilized as the medicine kicked in and her inner turmoil subsided.

With her disorder now under control, Charlotte finished high school, spent two years in a community college, and then transferred to a large state university. A few times she stopped her medication; each time irrepressible thoughts would return, and she had difficulty focusing. She was once arrested for threatening women outside an abortion

9: THE EX WITH PSYCHOLOGICAL PROBLEMS

clinic. But whenever Charlotte spun out of control, her parents stepped in and forced her to resume her medication and return to therapy. Then Charlotte would stabilize once more.

Charlotte eventually stabilized enough to earn a nursing degree. Then she met Robert and got pregnant. Charlotte and Robert decided to marry. Whether or not Charlotte ever told Robert before they wed that she was schizophrenic is unclear, but five years after Chloe was born, Robert filed for divorce because Charlotte's erratic behavior had become too much for him to take.

After they separated, Robert charged that Charlotte was an unfit mother. He said that she dragged Chloe along on subway rides to distant parts of the city. When she got there, she, with Chloe by her side, preached on street corners. He argued that Charlotte's schizophrenia, which became manifest each time she stopped her medication, ultimately put Chloe at risk. He asked for primary legal and physical custody.

Charlotte argued that Robert, until their separation, was mostly an absent parent. She, on the other hand, had worked part-time so that she could care for Chloe. Chloe was primarily attached to her, not to Robert. Charlotte acknowledged the problems that arose when she stopped taking her medications, but she also pointed out that she always stabilized once she resumed her treatment protocol.

A detailed custody evaluation confirmed that Chloe was indeed attached to Charlotte. It also revealed that not only was Robert relatively uninvolved with his daughter but also that he had little understanding of child development. Charlotte and Robert ultimately agreed that Chloe would do better if she had access to both her parents. They agreed to co-parent and that together they would make decisions about Chloe's life and future.

Their co-parenting agreement contained unusual clauses relating to Charlotte's mental health. Charlotte had to remain on her medication until her doctor indicated otherwise. Her psychiatrist, who managed that medication, and her psychotherapist had to check in each month with me, as the court-ordered parent coordinator, to confirm that she was following her treatment plan and showing no signs of schizophrenia. The agreement also stipulated that if Charlotte's mental health deteriorated, then I had quasi-judicial authority to grant Robert temporary custody until all professionals agreed that Charlotte was stable. Only once in the next four years, when Charlotte regressed, did I have to give Robert sole legal and physical custody. After several months in treatment, Charlotte was once again on an even keel, and she and Robert returned to the co-parenting arrangement. Perhaps out of fear of losing custody in the future, Charlotte has complied with her treatment protocol since then.

Mental disorders do not necessarily preclude a parent from effective co-parenting. At a minimum, parenting requires the capacity to care for your child's physical needs and to keep him safe from harm. Parenting means modeling good behavior for your child and effectively managing her behaviors. Parenting entails overseeing your child's emotional and physical development. Parenting means loving your child. Parents with emotional and psychological problems may not only love their children deeply but may also still be fully capable of providing for their needs. Meanwhile, the psychologically healthier parent can have absolutely no clue about how to parent effectively.

A diagnosis of depression or, as in Charlotte's case, schizophrenia, does not automatically mean you cannot co-parent. But, if your depression keeps you from getting out of bed most mornings to make breakfast and get your six-year-old off to school, then co-parenting puts your child at risk. However, if your depression is managed—if, because you know that mornings are hard for you, you compensate by making a bag lunch and setting out the breakfast cereal and fruit the night before; if you can get your child dressed, fed, and out the door to the school bus—then there is no reason why you cannot co-parent the child you love.

I once saw an attorney relentlessly hammer away at an anxious mother on the witness stand. He slammed her for taking antidepressants, claimed a depressive mother could not possibly be an effective parent, and smiled triumphantly as he reduced her to tears. The judge leaned forward and gently asked how much Prozac she was taking. "Ten milligrams, your honor." The judge responded, "Perhaps you should ask your doctor about a higher dosage. My wife has been doing much better on twenty milligrams." The judge then turned to the now red-faced attorney and asked "Any more questions in this area for this witness?"

No one is perfect. Everyone is flawed in some ways. As a co-parent, you need to remind yourself that you chose to have a child with this person. If he was an angry guy when you met and married, he is still going to be an angry guy now. If she had a mental illness, she will still have to deal with it, and so will you. You chose each other—flaws, strengths, and all. Moreover, your child has inherited characteristics from this person you once loved, later tolerated, and now may hate. Your ex becomes your child's co-parent, along with the set of flaws and strengths you know so well.

Maria was arrested after her terrified twelve-year-old son, Max, called the police from the front seat of her car. Maria had been racing through suburban streets, flying over speed bumps, and blowing past stop signs while cursing out Jorge, Max's father. Minutes later, when the police, with sirens shrieking, caught up with her, Maria's blood alcohol level of .23 was nearly three times the legal limit. She lost her license and the right to see her son for the immediate future. Jorge filed with the court to modify their co-parenting arrangement. He wanted

Maria to have only supervised visitation with Max. Before the hearing date, Maria checked into a drug and alcohol treatment program. When Jorge and Maria got to court, Maria showed letters from her treatment program attesting to her sobriety and affirming that she was dealing with her alcoholism through education and treatment. The court denied Jorge's petition and permitted Maria to resume co-parenting without external supervision.

About two months later, a loud crash woke Max in Maria's apartment. She was roaring drunk and was smashing plates and cups, picture frames, and mirrors. Petrified, Max called his father. The police arrived and handcuffed Maria after she resisted arrest. This time, the court awarded Jorge temporary legal and physical custody. Maria could see her son only for a few hours with a supervisor present and in a public place—at the shopping mall, the library or a local community center.

But after six months of sobriety, even though Maria had missed a number of supervised visitations, the court once again allowed her unsupervised contact with Max twice a week, but not overnight. It did so only after Maria installed in her car an interlock breathalyzer system with a zero tolerance for alcohol that would prevent her car from starting until she passed a breathalyzer test.

The alcoholic parent puts her child at risk. Not only is the child physically endangered, as was Max, but the child in the alcoholic family is emotionally undermined. Children need their parents to be consistent, caring, and focused on their needs. But the child of the alcoholic parent grows up in a world that is destabilized, where her father spirals out of control or where her mother smashes dishes and rants and raves. The child in the alcoholic family grows up before her time. She learns to be cautious, never carefree.

Co-parenting with an alcoholic is extremely difficult. Your ex's

9: THE EX WITH PSYCHOLOGICAL PROBLEMS

alcoholism impinges on your life. He does not keep his commitments. Her chaos and disorganization spill over into your world.

Still it is very important that your child maintain a relationship with your alcoholic ex. The court will need to set controls over how much time your child and ex spend together. The court may demand that all visits be supervised by family, friends, or even paid professionals. The court may order that your child not get into a car with your ex. If your ex falls off the wagon, visitation should be discontinued until your alcoholic ex can demonstrate once again that she has been going to Alcoholics Anonymous meetings or therapy.

Co-parenting with an ex who has a personality disorder is also extremely difficult. People with personality disorders display thoughts and feelings that are markedly deviant from societal norms. They may be rigid. They may fail to interpret and react appropriately to others. They may be emotionally intense and unable to control their impulses.

The parent with a personality disorder may be paranoid (distrusting and suspicious), schizoid (socially detached and hypersensitive), antisocial (hostile and disruptive) or narcissistic—utterly preoccupied with himself and lacking empathy for all others. When dating, individuals with personality disorders can be charismatic and alluring. But as exes, especially exes you co-parent with, they can make your life hell.

The ex with a personality disorder will turn your discussions about your child to herself and her perspectives. You think you are having a conversation about carpooling to a birthday party, but the conversation morphs into a rant about your failures as a spouse. No matter what the topic—your son's excellent report card, your daughter's upcoming ballet recital—your ex turns the conversation to your overwhelming shortcomings.

You know that co-parenting should run like a business. You know there is no profit in revisiting your failed marriage with your ex. You know that, to succeed in co-parenting, you and your ex must avoid conflict and focus together on appropriate decisions for your child. When your ex with the personality disorder deviates from the business plan, you must refocus attention onto your child. If your narcissistic ex demands you praise her accomplishments, focus on her strengths as a parent to your child. Remember, you could not resolve your ex's personality disorder when you were married. You cannot fix it now that you are apart. The key is to keep it focused on the child and his needs.

So how do you protect your child if your ex has a serious psychological problem? Basically by being the best parent you can be and serving as a positive role model. Children observe and imitate their parents. Honesty, integrity, and maturity will foster healthy development and offset the potential harmful influences of a dysfunctional parent. Love your child and allow your child to love both her parents freely. Adapt your parenting to your child's evolving development. Appropriately utilize rules and structure in your household, even if they are not matched by your ex. Encourage your child's independence. Treat your ex with respect. Help your child feel emotionally and behaviorally safe by setting appropriate boundaries, disciplining fairly, and consistently encouraging responsibility. Teach your child that he is not responsible for the behavior of either of his parents.

You may not always have the answer as to why Mommy drinks a lot or why Daddy gets so angry, but explain what you can at the child's level of understanding. Allow your child to honestly express her concerns. Demonstrate understanding and support for how difficult her situation sometimes must be.

Your child needs to maintain a relationship with both parents, even when one parent's imperfections go beyond the norm. Let your child maintain this relationship with your difficult ex, but rely upon friends, family, and community resources to insure that your child always remains safe.

Part Three

YOUR KID SAID
WHAT?

CHAPTER 10

"Hell No—I Won't Go!": Your Child Refuses Visitation

After they had divorced when their daughter was ten, Alexandra's parents lived in the same suburb. They had maintained an appropriate co-parenting relationship. They attended school events and doctor appointments together and, with the exception of some quarrels over money, were fairly cordial. Alexandra's mother continued, as she had before, to make most of the day-to-day decisions for her daughter, and Alexandra lived more of the time with her. Still, Alexandra saw her father frequently. She had her own room at his condo, and she spent every other weekend there. She saw her father at least once during the week, too.

Their co-parenting continued to function well even after Father moved to Texas when Alexandra was thirteen, where he took a new job and began a new relationship. Alexandra's co-parents crafted a revised schedule for her to see her dad. Alexandra flew to Texas every other month, whenever possible, during a long holiday weekend. The other months her father flew back to his old hometown to spend time with his daughter. Alexandra's co-parents also agreed she would spend several weeks in Texas during school vacations and summer breaks.

The first few times Alexandra flew to Texas for the weekend, she was excited. She enjoyed the freedom of traveling by herself and the new sights she saw with her father. She often bragged to her friends back home about her adventures. Likewise, the first few times her father came to visit, Alexandra really enjoyed the novelty of staying in a hotel, eating out for the entire weekend, and shopping at the mall with her dad.

But when the summer came and it was time for her to spend four weeks in Texas, it was a whole different story. Now Alexandra was living in her father's home, while he worked during the day, and her days were not anything like those earlier, intense short weekends focused on making certain she had a great time. Alexandra missed her friends and social network and was upset to be left out of the things they were doing "back home." She was bored. She also resented having to spend time with her father's girlfriend and her young children and that sometimes they used Alexandra as a babysitter.

The next October, when Alexandra was supposed to go to Texas over Columbus Day weekend, her soccer team was playing in a tournament, and Alexandra begged to stay home to play. Her parents agreed. A month later, her father's regular visit conflicted with plans Alexandra had made. Fall weekends meant an extra soccer practice for her school's team, plus this weekend she had a sleepover birthday party and she was expected, as usual, at church where she volunteered in the Sunday school. But her father insisted that after all the time, trouble, and expense he had undertaken to see his daughter, she must cancel her plans and spend the weekend with him.

Not surprisingly, Alexandra was crushed and then angry. She and her father argued much of the weekend. When he called her "a selfish brat," she stormed out of the hotel, called her mother to pick her up, and refused to see her father for the remainder of his visit.

Their next scheduled visit was during Christmas break. This time Alexandra flatly refused to get on the plane to Texas. She and her father argued again, and she hung up the phone on him. He then called back to accuse her mother of not insisting that Alexandra visit, and he threatened legal action to enforce their co-parenting plan. Mother accused Father of being verbally abusive, and their well-crafted co-parenting relationship unraveled. In the end Alexandra did not go to Texas that Christmas.

In January, her father flew in for his monthly visit. Alexandra agreed to meet him over lunch, where she told him that she was not going to Texas anymore and that whenever he flew in to see her, she would only have a few hours to spend with him. Her father exploded at Alexandra and also accused her mother of alienating his child. A family friend suggested that the two see a psychotherapist together. At first, Alexandra refused, but both her parents insisted. At the therapist's, Alexandra recalled several events from her childhood, some likely real and some surely imagined, where her father had been mean and aggressive toward her. She then announced that she would no longer have any contact with him.

Again her father threatened legal action against her mother; after all, he could not sue his daughter. Alexandra became furious. From there on in, she refused to talk to her father on the phone. She returned his letters and cards but only after she had scrawled on the envelope "sender unknown." He sent her a birthday present; she never opened it. A year after her father had moved to Texas, what had been a good father-daughter connection and a solid co-parenting relationship had totally deteriorated.

At some point in the future, the child of divorce may rebel against the visitation schedule you, your ex, and your lawyers spent so much time and money constructing. This rarely occurs, especially with younger children, in the first months after divorce. While you and your ex were divorcing, you clashed over your child's living arrangements. But by the time the divorce is finalized, your child will actually be relieved that the battle is over and that he no longer finds himself the focus of all the parental attention. He may be so emotionally exhausted and weary from the conflict that he willingly goes along with whatever you and your ex agreed. Your child is, just as you are, ready to put the strife of divorce behind him and move on with his life. Consequently, he accedes without a struggle to the new living arrangements you and your ex worked out. He wants his life once again to revolve around school, sports, and friends; not money, moves, lawyers, and courts. So for the first year or two after the divorce, the living arrangements you assembled so carefully work out as planned, with only occasional hiccups.

But eventually the calendar of his "visitations" becomes complicated, and the child begins to push back. There are two possible situations that lead to some children, a few years after the fireworks of divorce end, resisting going to one co-parent's home.

One is when the child becomes a pawn in the ongoing conflict between the co-parents and is pushed to choose sides. The child may react by refusing to spend time with one of her co-parents.

Other push-backs calling for changes to visitation are actually appropriate for a developing child and are an inevitable, though certainly not a welcome, manifestation of your child's growth. That's because your child's needs, desires, and expectations change as they mature; the living arrangements so carefully put together for an eight-year-old will not work for an adolescent.

When your child was younger, he entered into the routines of your life. When you were cooking dinner in the kitchen, he played with the pots and pans. When she grew older, she did her homework at the table while you stirred the soup and made the salad. When it snowed, you two made a game out of shoveling the driveway.

But as your child enters adolescence, the ground rules for her spending time with both of her co-parents change, just as they do for the child of an intact family. You need to understand this shift and adapt to it. If, as a co-parent, you want to have an effective relationship with your child as she grows into an adolescent and beyond, you are going to have to adjust to the new reality and follow a new rule of centering your time with your child on your child's life, even if it means that you lose some of your precious "visitation" time.

To be sure, Alexandra's father should not let his daughter command their relationship. As her co-parent, he not only has the right to set its parameters, but his needs must be considered, too. However, he did not shift to co-parenting an adolescent. He needed to center his time with his child around the child's life. Alexandra's father utterly failed to consider what his developing child needed. The problem surfaced that first summer in Texas. He should have made plans for her that would have introduced her to new friends and given her something fun and interesting to do. He could have found a soccer camp where she could have honed her skills. She would then have returned to her home team a stronger player. He could have let her try something she had never tried before—a week for teens at a cooking school or volunteering with underprivileged children. He should have investigated possibilities for occupying a thirteen-year-old, not left her to her own devices.

Then, when he arrived on the weekend she had so many plans, he should have entered into her life. He should have said that, of course, she could not possibly miss her team's practice. Certainly, he, like any parent, would drive her to and from the practice. Perhaps they could grab a bite afterward. Would she mind if he stayed to watch the practice, since he never was there for games? He could have said, "Can we have dinner before the birthday sleepover? Or since I am in town only this weekend, could I pick you up from the sleepover at 10:00 instead of at 11:00, and we'll get pancakes?" He should not have asked her to skip her volunteer time at the church. But he could have entered into the event, not only by driving her there—which, after all, is a major component of the life of any parent of an adolescent without a driver's license—but also by offering to see if there was a way he could help out while she worked with her class. Alexandra's father could have tried to connect with his adolescent daughter by centering their time together around her life and needs, not his life and desires.

Giving In Is Not Giving Up

Face it: having to switch houses every other weekend has become a real drag for your teenaged daughter. Look at it from her point of view. It's Friday night; that means Mom drives her to Dad's house, but your daughter has other plans for the weekend: she wants to spend it with her friends. She wants to go to the football game and party afterward, and then six girls are having a sleepover. Everyone is going to Stacy's house; she has a huge basement, big-screen TV, and room enough for six to sleep over—and you don't. Stacy's house is cool; yours is not. She cannot possibly miss all that just to spend time with one of her parents.

Don't take it personally; she's not rejecting you and your house because she wants to spend time with her other parent. It's not because she doesn't love you. She simply wants to stay in the neighborhood that will allow her to hang out with her weekday friends. Even if you readily provide all the transportation and communication tools to connect her to those friends and her meaningful weekday world, during adolescence parents are a necessary interruption in the flow of her weekend.

While she certainly can Facebook, text, and Tweet from your house as well, she is being moved out of her comfort zone. She fears that at your place she will be passed over. Even if you do the good divorced parent thing and invite her friends to join the two of you, she is still not going to want to do it.

Adolescents are learning their own minds and making their own choices. Conflicts between parents and adolescents are normal and healthy. Adolescents test limits and take risks; parents establish boundaries and seek safety. Adolescents are energetic, strong, and sometimes reckless. Parents are growing physically weaker and considerably more cautious. These natural generational conflicts, which can be difficult in any family, can become aggravated for those co-parenting a child of divorce. Post-divorce parents must enter into the life of the child, rather than expect the child to enter their lives. In an intact family, the child does not have a choice: "This is what our family does." But in divorce situations, your adolescent does have an option—stay with the other parent.

If soccer or church is important to your child, become a part of that activity rather than fighting for your independent life with your child. If you, as co-parent, prioritize your desires over those of your child, you will lose. You may insist that your adolescent, while she is staying with you, babysit for the children of your new girlfriend, but unless your daughter wants to do this, she will resent you for making her take on this chore and will perhaps choose not to see you as often.

Living arrangements that worked for the co-parents for years now change. Academic, social, and extracurricular commitments will alter accustomed patterns. Your adolescent no longer wants to spend every other weekend shifting homes or sleeping over on Wednesday nights. Once your adolescent drives, he may say, "How about if I come by Sunday afternoon and we'll watch the football game together." Homework and basketball practice will put an end to your Tuesday night dinners at the hamburger joint. Remember, every other night of the week, he feels free to chow down his meal and then ask to be excused to finish his algebra homework and the first draft of the English essay due tomorrow.

Adjusting the times you and your child spend together does not mean changing your co-parenting responsibilities. To parent successfully the adolescent of divorce, both co-parents must continue to agree on how to manage the unbridled enthusiasms of their adolescent. Shifting the times and places you see your adolescent child does not mean abrogating your responsibility for making sound decisions about her life.

Many adolescents will not want to move back and forth from house to house. There is no point in challenging this by throwing in the child's face—or in the face of your ex—a copy of the court order issued when your child was seven. Instead you must try, with your ex and adolescent, to identify the problem. Why doesn't your adolescent want to spend time at your home? As you explore the problem, consider how this change will affect everyone involved: not just you, your ex, and your child, but also your other children, your child's stepsiblings, extended family, and even friends.

As you explore options, remember that schedule changes do not have to be permanent or codified. Nearly all parenting agreements allow co-parents to modify them if they both agree. You can be flexible, saying: "Let's move away from our scheduled dinners on Thursdays from 5:00 to 8:00 p.m. Instead, can we speak on Sunday evening to look at the week ahead and see if there is a night we can get together for dinner and to catch up?" You can then say: "Let's try this system for six weeks. When the time is up, let's see if it works; let's try to see each other every week, even if only for a short time."

Entering the life of your adolescent rather than insisting that she enter yours does not mean you give up. It just means that you have become realistic. You understand that your adolescent is no longer a child; he wants less time with you than he once did. He now has other important relationships that take precedence, as they should. However, that does not mean that he no longer needs you. You remain his co-parent even if you and he spend less time together than you—although not your child—would wish.

Understand what your adolescent is feeling. She has had enough of all the changes your divorce has brought to her life. Her friends don't switch houses every few days. Her friends don't have to plan ahead to make sure to pack the cute top to wear to the movies on Friday night. Her friends don't have to deal with a different set of rules at Dad's house and a different curfew at Mom's house.

You Are Still the Parent. Act Like One.

Should you support your adolescent when he refuses to see your ex? Absolutely not! Though an adolescent saying she does not want to do something with her parents is hardly a novel experience, nevertheless both of the co-parents have the right to spend time with their adolescent. Adolescents have the right to have some control in scheduling where and when they see their co-parents, but they cannot refuse to see one or the other.

If you give any signal that validates your child's refusal to see your ex, your child will pounce on your permission. If you say, "Gee, his anger sounds like what it was when we were married," your son will read that as your saying he need not see his father. If, when your adolescent heads off reluctantly for a visit, you say: "Be safe; call me if there is a problem," you have intimated that you expect a problem. Do not confuse the problems you had when you were married to your ex with your child's relationship with that co-parent.

Just as you would not let your adolescent stay out all night with her boyfriend or ignore her homework, so too you should not condone or allow her to end her relationship with one of her parents. The key to raising a successful child of divorce is for that child to have solid relationships with both co-parents, even when those relationships are naturally strained by the emotional storms of adolescence. Just as you help your adolescent figure out a workable plan for attacking all that homework, so too you may help him decide when is the best time to see your ex.

But how they spend that time—with Dad watching practice from the sidelines or with Mom driving from the basketball game to church choir practice—is up for grabs. The important thing is for both co-parents to send the same message: that each co-parent and child must spend some time together every week.

Hayley came into my office seeking advice for her son Austin, who refused to spend time with his father. Hayley said she wanted Austin to spend time with his dad, but then she began to list all the things she did not like about her ex and his interactions with Austin. Dad didn't take Austin to church; his idea of dinner was a hamburger and fries from McDonald's; Dad never bothered to check if Austin had done his homework. Austin knew how his mom felt. Her message to Austin was clear: spend time with your father and you will be ungodly, unhealthy, and uneducated.

Sometimes your child worries about you when she is with her other parent. Do not reinforce her worries. Don't send her off to Dad's saying how much you will miss her. Don't welcome her home with how lonely you were all weekend while she was away. Your child is not supposed to take care of your needs; you are supposed to take care of her. Your message should be simple: "Have a great time at your dad's."

10: "HELL NO—I WON'T GO!" YOUR CHILD REFUSES VISITATION

If she asks what you are going to do this weekend, be specific about some of your plans. You will be catching up on work, doing your taxes, having lunch with a friend. In other words, you will be doing some adult activities you cannot always do when she's around. Your child should understand that your life continues when she is with her other parent and that you are fine with this. When she returns, don't frown and smirk when she gushes on about the things she did with your ex. Smile, ask appropriate questions, and actively support this relationship.

Don't let your feelings toward your ex interfere with your child's healthy relationship with this parent. If your child refuses to see your ex, your child might be thinking of you and your needs. He may be trying to please you. If your child refuses to see your ex, don't feed into this behavior. It is not good for your child; it is not good for you.

You must make a sustained effort to enter into the life of your child in order to maintain a relationship with her. That relationship may not always be what you want it to be. Understand that your adolescent has her own life and has options. Both you and your child change over time. Allow your relationship to change as well.

CHAPTER 11

"She's Moving Out—and In with Him!"

Jake and Emma met at a downtown bar when both were fairly young. Emma, a college student from a middle-class family, liked that Jake was so different from the guys in polo shirts and khakis she met at school. Jake, a construction worker, had the biceps of a man who earned his living as a laborer and the tattoos that were a mark of manhood in his circle of buddies who, most nights, met for a few beers and to watch a ball game or play video games. Jake and Emma were both from large Catholic families; they had that in common, but it was their differences that attracted each to the other.

Emma got pregnant, and Jake and Emma announced their plans to marry. Neither family really wanted that; but when the possibility of an abortion was raised, Emma, with years of Catholic school behind her, adamantly refused. Jake and Emma had a small wedding, and Emma completed her third year of college before the baby arrived. She planned, after the baby was born, to return for her senior year, but because Jake forgot to put his son Mason on the waiting list at the college daycare center as soon as he was born, Emma had no child care for her senior year. Jake's mother offered to watch the baby so Emma could finish school, but Emma, remembering how much Jake's parents had opposed her marriage, declined. She stayed home to care for Mason.

Meanwhile, marriage and fatherhood had not changed Jake much. After work, he still hung out with his buddies drinking, betting on ball games, and playing video games. Jake did provide financially for his new family, but his taking a turn with child care was not part of the package. He thought he made real changes. He worked more overtime, and he cut back on how often he went out with his friends drinking during the week. Nevertheless, by Mason's first birthday, Emma and Jake, realizing just how incompatible they were, separated.

Jake's parents feared they would be cut off from their grandchild. They pushed Jake to seek custody of the toddler. Instead the court ruled joint legal custody and co-parenting for Jake and Emma. Mason lived primarily with Emma, but Jake had daytime visitations every other weekend. Jake never "got" parenting. He moved into a group apartment with his buddies, a setup utterly unsuited to Mason spending the night. He would forget to feed Mason. He plopped Mason in front of a monitor to play video games for hours on end.

It didn't take long for Mason to react to the inadequate care. When Jake came to pick up Mason, Mason would cling to his mother, and his visits with Mason became shorter; sometimes Jake just visited Mason at Emma's apartment.

Their immature but workable co-parenting arrangement endured as long as Jake didn't push for much more contact. But the agreement was structured to give Jake a much greater role in his son's life once Mason entered school and was ready to be separated from his mother for longer periods of time. Emma initially agreed that starting

11: "SHE'S MOVING OUT—AND IN WITH HIM!"

the summer before Mason entered first grade he would live primarily with his father during the summers when school was not in session. But when Mason was finishing kindergarten and Jake told Emma that he was expecting his son to spend the summer with him, she began to object. From what she knew of Mason's weekends with his father, she argued that Jake was not suited to raise her son, especially since he had not kept Mason on a regular eating or sleeping schedule during their bimonthly visits. She filed a motion to change the custody agreement to block Mason from taking her son for the summer, and to make her case stronger, she charged that her ex was an alcoholic.

However, by this time Jake had remarried, and his new wife was staying at home with their infant. Jake argued that he was not an alcoholic and that he had maintained a solid relationship with his son during his weekend visitations. Emma lost her court battle, and Mason went to spend the summer with his father and his new family.

But the bad blood between the former spouses caused their co-parenting agreement to effectively collapse, as they both actively criticized and condemned everything they could about each other's parenting styles. Jake thought Emma was making a sissy out of their son because she would not let him play flag football. Emma thought Jake exposed Mason to inappropriate movies and video games. Communication between the parents so deteriorated that they made contact only via terse emails or through Mason. During the school year Emma made all the academic, social, and medical decisions for her son; during the summers Jake or his wife handled most of the decision making for the boy. Jake and Emma continued to muddle through Mason's co-parenting, turning every so often to the court to help resolve issues.

It was a powder keg of opposition and conflict. One day, when Mason was eleven and Jake and his wife left him home alone to babysit his younger half sister, that keg exploded. While his father and stepmother were out, Mason heard some noises outside and got scared. He called his mother. Emma called the police and Child Protective Services, claiming that Jake had neglected and endangered Mason. Once again, she went to court to change custody and the visitation schedule so that Mason would not spend most of the summer with his father. Although the court chastised Jake for leaving an eleven-year-old home alone with a younger child, the judge did not change the custody arrangement. Emma disapproved of Jake's behavior, but Mason really loved being with his dad. Jake had matured somewhat since his failed marriage. Jake and Mason played football and basketball together. They hiked in the mountains and fished in a nearby river. They worked together on rebuilding an old sports car Jake bought at auction, and Mason fantasized about one day in the future when he would be sitting behind the wheel. Jake didn't nag Mason about getting his schoolwork done. He figured that was Emma's job.

Mason blew up when he learned his mother had filed in court to limit his time with his dad. Emma's explanations didn't help Mason feel any better. Mason took away the message that his mom didn't want him to see his dad. Mason was pissed.

Then, when Mason was in eighth grade, a new stepfather and a new baby came into his life. Feeling displaced within his own home and encouraged by Jake, Mason asked to live with his father for high school. Emma refused. As she and Mason argued one night, she slapped him. Mason walked out of the house and called his father. Now Jake filed a motion to change primary residence, claiming Emma was an abusive, unfit parent.

The court ordered Jake and Emma into mediation. Emma understood that Mason wanted to experience what life was like living with his father full time and not just for summer vacations. But she feared that if she gave in, Mason would later resent her for not fighting for him when, as she fully expected, he changed his mind and wanted to come home to her. She worried if she said yes now, a year from now, when Mason would change his mind, Jake would not let him return to her home. With the help of their attorneys and a parent coordinator, Emma and Jake were finally convinced to let Mason live with Jake and spend his freshman year in his father's neighborhood high school. Both accepted that, at the end of that school year, all parties would reassess the situation for the future.

Mason found living with his father during ninth grade relatively uneventful. He frequently saw his mother during the week, but, without Emma "on him" all the time about schoolwork, his academic performance declined. The high school in his father's neighborhood was much larger than the schools he was used to, and Mason neither made good friends there nor got much playing time on its competitive freshman football team. By May of his freshman year, without much encouragement from Emma, Mason told his father that, while he really loved being with him during the school year, he wanted to return to his mother's house, to spend the rest of high school in that smaller and less competitive setting with his old friends. Both Emma and Jake accepted Mason's request. They also rearranged Mason's summer that year so that he spent half his time at his father's home and half at his mother's.

Now a freshman in college, Mason considers that experience in ninth grade a success. Although he was often unhappy that year, had almost no friends, and failed to develop good study habits, he learned something else, something very important. He learned what it was really like to live with his father and his family. No longer would Mason idolize the parent he did not live with most of the time. And he was allowed to grow in his understanding of his father, his mother, and himself in his own way, through his own search and his own journey. With high school behind him, Mason now understood: "Ninth grade sucked, but I wouldn't have traded it for anything. I don't have to wonder for the rest of my life what might have been different if I had lived with my dad or what it would have been like. I now know what it was like. It was okay, and I don't have to think about it forever."

Jake and Emma made many mistakes as co-parents. Their conflict post-separation and post-divorce was more intense and lasted far longer than their short marriage. They did not shelter Mason from the conflict. They did not make decisions jointly; instead each took full control of Mason during the time he lived with them. When they could not agree, they turned right away to the court to resolve issues. Still, Mason had what is primary for children of divorce—a regular, consistent, ongoing relationship with both co-parents. Ultimately both Jake and Emma listened to their son; they allowed him to choose to live with his father for ninth grade and to return to his mother's home after that. Mason thus experienced living full time with both his parents, and he understood how each loved him.

Mason also saw his parents struggle and eventually succeed as co-parents. Together Emma and Jake decided that Mason would live with Jake for ninth grade and that he could move back to Emma's to finish high school. These difficult parenting decisions changed the exes' pattern of conflict and of turning to the court to intervene every time they could not agree on how to parent Mason. Resolving where Mason would live allowed Jake and Emma to make other parenting decisions together for their son. Over time, they agreed on curfews, driving rules, homework responsibilities, summer jobs, and college.

It is quite common, even in healthy co-parenting relationships that are relatively free from strife, for a teenager to ask to change his living arrangements. Teens do this not to punish one parent or because they idolize the other, but rather out of a legitimate yearning to understand

11: "SHE'S MOVING OUT—AND IN WITH HIM!"

what it is like to live with the other co-parent—just like in an intact family—day in and day out. Weekend visitations, holidays, and summer vacations do not provide sufficient time for the teenager, whose identity is in flux, to form a full picture of the parent she sees less often. If all your child's contacts with your ex take place during the freedom of holidays and weekends, your child will wonder what is it like to live in that house when he has to rush off to school and Mom has to get out the door to work. Your child wants to experience this kind of "regular" living with the co-parent.

This desire might become especially pronounced after your child becomes empowered by the independence of a driver's license. Now your adolescent may come to you with a plan. He has figured out that he can live with Dad for senior year without any disruptions. He will take a flex first-period class. That means he won't have to get up any earlier at Dad's house in order to make it into his regular high school on time. Since he won't have to change schools, friends, athletics, or his social life, the only alteration in his life will be the house where he sleeps. Since he drives and has use of a car, he can drop by Mom's whenever he wants. He knows he will need to see her to get help with his schoolwork and his college applications. Everything will stay the same except that the child can, at last, see what it is really like to live with his father. Although he may not even realize it consciously or completely, for your child, living with his dad is an attempt to integrate that relationship fully into his life before he heads out into the wider world.

Your child may also be at a stage of development where she is just trying to figure out her adolescent identity. Your daughter may not admit it, but she may want to live with her mother partly to see what it's like to be an adult woman. Your son wants to spend more time with his father to see what it's like to be a man. Your adolescent probably won't be able to articulate this clearly. He won't say, "I want to live with Dad so I can learn to be a guy." Instead he'll say, "Mom, I can't stand being around you all the time." The words are different, but the meaning is the same.

If You Love Your Child, Let Him Go

As painful as this switch may be to one of the parents, to your adolescent it is extremely important. Your adolescent is not ending the relationship you two have had. Rather, your adolescent seeks another perspective to carry with him into his future—a real, day-by-day relationship with his other co-parent. You may worry that all the things you hate about your ex will rub off on your child if she lives in his house. But by the last years of high school, you have already taught your child the work habits, morals, and values you want to pass on. Your child has internalized them, and you need not fear that, just because your child lives with your ex, your child's attitudes and behaviors will shift 180 degrees.

Let your child go. She may discover that all those negative perceptions about your ex that you so subtly had imparted over the years are true. Or he may discover that your ex is now a very different person from the one you once knew and that he has much to learn from this co-parent. That learning will augment—but not replace—what you have already taught your child.

Transitions in living arrangements are not feasible for every family of divorce. In some families the living arrangements for the child were more evenly balanced all along. In others, logistics, like distance to school or the lack of accessible transportation, make a change impractical. But if your adolescent asks to make a switch and it seems possible to meet her request, consider not just your feelings of rejection but also what your child may gain from living more of the time with her other co-parent.

11: "SHE'S MOVING OUT—AND IN WITH HIM!"

It is your responsibility to make sure that your child really wants to change his living arrangements and is not just seeking temporary escape. When he says, "I hate you, I'm going to live with Mom" after he failed a geometry test and you took away his electronics for a week, that's not real. Do not permit your child to run away from your parenting. But you should let your child explore why he wants to live with your ex.

You need to discuss how moving means many changes—a new school, new friends, different extracurricular activities. Your child must understand the considerable impact of the move. When your marriage ended, you and your ex focused on the ramifications and impact of the change on your child. Now, as your child faces another possible change in living arrangements, you, your ex, and your child must review the impacts of this change.

CHAPTER 12

Don't Believe Everything Your Child Says

Melissa went ballistic when she overheard her children, seven-year-old Andrew and five-year-old Brad, complaining about eating their father's food when they were at his house during his two days a week and alternating weekends of visitation.

The boys were playing the "yucky foods" game in their mom's yard, calling weeds and grass "Daddy's food" and making believe they were throwing up. An anxious Melissa carefully questioned the boys. They said all they had been eating at Dad's house was broccoli, and they were going to puke.

Melissa quickly began to put two and two together, and she came up with an exaggerated, catastrophe scenario. Recently Melissa had taken Scott to court over child support, and she knew Scott was financially strapped. Already angry at Scott over money issues, Melissa believed everything she overheard while her children played. She never bothered to check the facts. When she heard her children complaining about the food, she assumed it meant that Scott could not afford to feed them adequately when they were at his house and was therefore jeopardizing their health and nutrition. She promptly shot off an email to her attorney accusing Scott of not properly feeding the children. Her lawyer then sent a letter to Scott's lawyer. Its gist: if Scott didn't have the financial wherewithal to feed his children, Melissa would be seeking a change in custody and living arrangements.

A defensive Scott never bothered to reply about what he was feeding his kids. Instead he countered that Melissa was attempting to alienate his sons. The truth was lost in the tumult, accusations, and counteraccusations.

What was the truth? Actually, Scott's neighbor had a bumper crop of broccoli that summer. She had given Scott a shopping bag filled with the vegetable. Scott, honing his limited culinary skills and admittedly trying to save some money, had found a number of broccoli recipes on the Internet. He had indeed fed his sons broccoli for a few days: cream of broccoli soup, chicken and broccoli Chinese style, even broccoli and cheese. Scott himself was sick of all the broccoli and had even joked about it with the boys.

But what should have been a laughing matter between two parents who loved their sons turned into a heated conflict between the exes. Melissa believed everything the boys told her. The children reacted to Melissa's concerns and exaggerated them to try to please her. Scott responded with anger, and the parents failed to communicate effectively.

Don't believe everything your child tells you about the other parent or behaviors at the other parent's house. So many phone calls to attorneys and emergency court motions have been filed to modify or eliminate visitation because a child reported, "Daddy didn't feed me any dinner." Often there is some element of truth to this, but the child is saying this primarily to ally with the other parent. Maybe they did not

12: DON'T BELIEVE EVERYTHING YOUR CHILD SAYS

have dinner as you define it, with everyone sitting at a table together. Maybe they had a late lunch that day. Maybe they just went out for snacks. Maybe your daughter just refused to eat. Your intense reactions to those comments, however, are reinforcing. Emails are fired off and calls are placed to attorneys, bonding the child with you amid a tremendous amount of energy generated by that simple comment.

You have a right to raise concerns about your children with your ex. Whether your concerns are about broccoli, bedtime, or homework, as a co-parent you must not keep silent. Parallel parenting means: I do in my household with my children what I want to do; you do in your household with your children what you want. But you are not a parallel parent; you are a co-parent. You and your ex are raising the same children. You want them to grow up to be respectful, independent, functioning individuals. You do not want them to become confused by conflicting demands. Both parents must decide together on the influences, structures, and controls of their child's life.

So don't come out of the corral with guns blasting. Don't accuse your ex of egregious behaviors based only on what you think your child has reported. Don't open with, "How dare you feed our children broccoli for every meal? You are an incompetent parent." Instead, say, "Our children raised something I need to share. They say they're sick of eating broccoli. I know they hate spinach. What's going on with the broccoli?"

If you are the co-parent on the receiving end of this query, your response should be nondefensive and nonjudgmental. Don't immediately accuse your ex of trying to alienate your child. Maybe your son truly is sick of broccoli. Maybe you have not heard his complaints. Or maybe your child is just trying to pit one parent against the other.

Respond openly. "Yeah, we've been eating lots of broccoli. My neighbor gave us a bunch. To tell you the truth, I'm pretty sick of it myself, but it was good, free, and we're nearly done with it." That's where the conversation ends. You convey information, express concerns, and get feedback. Sometimes your ex won't be able to respond to your concerns immediately. If the concern is a child staying up too late, it's okay to say: "Thanks for telling me Rachel is listening to her iPod after lights out when she should be sleeping. I'll talk to her about the importance of getting enough sleep and will check up on her this week. I'll let you know more when we talk later."

It's important for your child to know his parents communicate regularly. She should know there really aren't any secrets about her between her parents. You both love her and you are both raising her. You need to know her worries and deal with them. Don't yell at your child for talking about the broccoli. Instead, say, "Mom told me you were sick of broccoli. I'm sick of it too, but what are we going to do when our neighbor brings over another bag of it next week?" Set up an environment that allows your child to talk freely to you about the broccoli and everything else. Ask yourself why he didn't tell you about hating the broccoli. Whether or not your child eats too much broccoli will not have a lasting effect on his life. Fighting over the broccoli with your ex, however, can hurt your child forever.

What Your Child Really Wants and Needs

Your young child develops with the belief that no matter what, she is able to trust the world around her. She can take her first steps, try new foods that taste yucky, get a shot at the pediatrician's office, stay with the baby sitter, and attend school, all because she trusts you. Divorce breaks that primary trust. Mothers and fathers are always supposed to love each other. Separation forces your child to question if she will always be loved as well. Such uncertainty is painful to your child and

12: DON'T BELIEVE EVERYTHING YOUR CHILD SAYS

she will attempt to return to homeostasis, the state of the family life prior to the separation. Her immediate goal is reunification, getting her parents back together. Even if the marriage was filled with strife, tension, and disagreement, your family stress was what she was used to, and her goal is to return to that status. Attempts fail, and the reunification becomes a fantasy. Attempts by one parent to castigate and blame the other challenges the reunification fantasy and leaves the child confused.

In an attempt to reunify her parents, your child will exaggerate the truth or create her versions of it. While it is rare for your child to actually say, "Mommy, Daddy said he misses you very much and is sorry he was angry with you," many children think of saying that. Roles reverse, and your child becomes sensitive to your needs, feeling that if she pleases either parent, reunification may occur.

Therefore she will often tell you what she thinks you want to hear. Pleasing parents secures her role in family life. She fears if Mom and Dad, who once loved each other, can separate and hate each other, they can hate her and leave her as well. By pleasing and allying with each parent, she tries to ensure the safety of her status and continued relationship with each parent. She will tell each parent what she thinks that parent wants to hear. Very quickly her remarks include things about your ex that are not necessarily the truth. If you complained the marriage ended because of your ex's anger, you will soon begin to hear your child describe similar angry episodes. There may be elements of truth to the report, but likely they are exaggerated. Your child is telling you what she thinks you want to hear about your ex and is telling the other parent what she thinks that parent wants to hear. This is self-preservation. "Mom left Dad. If I disagree with Mom she might leave me as well." Your child tells you what she thinks you want to hear. "I know it was my fault Mom left Dad. They were always arguing about me. If I agree with Mom that Dad is always angry when I'm with him, then it really wasn't my fault."

Parents tend to react to their child's reports of their ex as if they were gospel. Why? Because the reports reinforce the parental perception of the other parent, justify the parents' worries, and assuage any possible guilt.

Changes in life circumstances cause many parents to question their decisions to separate. Reinforcement by the child of the behavior that led to the separation ensures the parent that she did the correct thing. Reports by the child that reinforce the parental decision are encouraged. Parents think, "See? He still is angry; that's why I left."

The goal is to help your child move away from thoughts of reunification and self-blame and away from the focus on your needs toward a focus on school, friends, and her personal self-growth issues.

An effective co-parenting arrangement reduces the intensity of the child saying what she thinks the parent wants to hear. If the parents support each other's role in the life of the child, communicate directly with each other regularly in a businesslike fashion about their child, and don't reinforce the child for saying what she thinks the parent wants, the child can be honest in her report, deal with her elements of self-blame, and decrease the intensity of the reunification fantasy.

Part Four

TILL DEATH DO YOU CO-PARENT

CHAPTER 13

Breaking Up Your Breakup

Jack and Cheryl had divorced two years ago when their son, Tommy, was seven and their daughter, Lucy, just five. The marriage had ended because Jack was an alcoholic, and he was abusive to Cheryl. The children, even at those young ages, could remember a drunken Jack falling asleep on the couch and the times when he had become explosive and belligerent. Like many children of alcoholics, Tommy and Lucy had learned to read Jack's mood and to avoid him when he sipped "Daddy's special soda" after dinner every night.

During the divorce proceedings, Jack agreed to weekend daytime visitations with the children. However, a year later, he acquired a new girlfriend, and, thinking that with her he could certainly handle the kids, he petitioned the court for overnight stays. Cheryl's attorney told her that she had no chance of blocking the motion: Jack had no criminal record, had never been arrested for driving under the influence of alcohol, and his string of job changes was common for someone in the information technology consulting industry. The court granted Jack overnight visitation every other weekend.

Cheryl was, understandably, deeply concerned about the children getting in the car with Jack when he had been drinking. She hit upon a ruse. For their overnights the kids would bring their favorite DVDs to Jack's house and ask him for a movie night. They spent their bimonthly Saturday evenings watching DVDs and eating pizza that had been delivered. The scheme worked for several months until the day the children came home reporting that Jack and his girlfriend began drinking their special soda after lunch and that Jack had beaten up his girlfriend.

Visitation transitions became confusing and unpredictable. Sometimes Jack's girlfriend would pick the children up in her car. Then, two or three times, Jack came to pick the children up in a taxi. The first time, he said his car had been in an accident and was being repaired. The next time he showed up in a taxi, he said the car was back in the shop because of a defective part. The time after that he said it was in the auto body shop waiting for the paint to dry.

Then Jack moved to an apartment in the center of their exurban community where he could walk to grocery and convenience stores and board the major lines of public transportation. Jack told the children and Cheryl that, with gas prices rising, he had decided to sell his car, use public transportation, and, when he needed to do so, take taxis as he did to pick up his children for their weekend visitation. However, when the children reported to Cheryl that they had spotted what they thought was their dad's car in the garage of his apartment complex—they recognized its stickers—she became suspicious. A search of county police records revealed that Jack had been arrested months prior for driving while intoxicated, that he had lost his license, and that subsequently he had gone to jail after he was arrested a second time for drunk driving with a suspended license.

Jack had lied and misled Cheryl and the children for months. He had once again broken the children's foundational trust. They would no longer sleep at Jack's home, but Cheryl did not want all contact to end. She agreed to take them to his apartment for lunch on alternate weekends. However, after Jack showed up drunk at Tommy's Little League game, the children refused further contact. Jack, who claimed that he had been too embarrassed to tell Cheryl and the children about his arrests, entered a court-ordered substance abuse treatment program. Still the children refused any further contact with their father.

We know that children derive great benefit from co-parenting. What is unquestionably best for most children is for both of their parents to be involved, without conflict, in their lives. If you and your ex can achieve this ideal, if you two can work past your differences to make the right decisions needed to raise your child, then your child can recover that fundamental trust that was first broken in the divorce, and together you and your ex can launch your child into adulthood equipped with the toolkit needed to thrive and succeed in the world.

But there are times when co-parenting will not work or must not work. Families do exist in which it is in your child's paramount interest to maintain primary attachment to only one parent and to forego meaningful contact with the other. The case of Jack and Cheryl is one such sad example.

Jack's alcoholism led to erratic and dangerous behavior that made it impossible for a valuable and safe relationship with his children to continue. Not until Jack evidenced signs of long-term sobriety and worked at repairing his relationship with his son and daughter could co-parenting be contemplated.

Parents with substance abuse problems fail as co-parents, because their drinking and drugging interfere with their judgment and reasoning. Unable to control their own behavior, they cannot make sound decisions for their child.

But addictions are not the only problems that could rule out co-parenting. We saw in an earlier chapter how mental issues could lead to problems with co-parenting, and how many of these issues could be resolved. And even the worst of attitudes and personal animosities can sometimes be overcome, as we have seen throughout this book.

In most cases of successful co-parenting, the co-parents can recall times of trust and caring from the past. Both will recall their joy at the birth of their child, his first words, her first steps, and how together they sat up all night in a steamy bathroom when he had the croup. When co-parents can reinterpret these memories, not as moments reflecting their own previous intimacy, but rather as reference points for how much they both cared for their child, the likelihood of their co-parenting effectively increases.

However, some co-parents have such a dysfunctional relationship that they cannot move to the necessary stage of parenting their child together. There are situations in which the chronic nature of the conflict prevents the ability to co-parent, in which the conflict predates the parental separation for so many years that it is impossible for the parents to interact without conflict.

When their conflict has existed for so long that the parents cannot recall anything but chronic mistrust and anger, co-parenting will fail. If, after the divorce, tensions between the co-parents do not diminish, if the level of hostility remains so high that your child feels he is still living in your divorce war zone, then co-parenting may have to be abandoned. If your child sees that others—therapists, family members, lawyers, judges, parent coordinators—are making all the decisions in his life because his co-parents cannot agree, then, for the sake of the child, joint legal custody has to be abandoned in favor of sole custody. The child will then live with one parent and visit the other sometimes. The custodial parent will have the right to make all decisions affecting the child's life and future; the noncustodial parent will not have input to control those decisions.

But remember: even if you have sole legal custody, you should support contact and any positive feelings and attachments between your child and your ex. Substance abuse, psychological problems, or past physical maltreatment of your child may limit your ex's opportunities to see your child. He may need to have a supervisor present when they visit. She may see her child only once a month. However, the important point remains unchanged: your ex is still your child's parent. In most situations it is healthier for your child to continue to have some kind of a relationship with both parents. It is your job, as the parent with sole custody, to support the positive aspects in this relationship; you must do it for your child's sake. Parent your child without denigrating your ex so that your child can enjoy the time she spends with your ex.

Over time, your child will come to understand the physical and emotional limitations of that relationship on her own. Find other supportive individuals—extended family members, teachers, local church or community organization leaders—to fill in some of what your child misses by not having his mom or dad around much.

Don't Even Think About Co-Parenting When . . .

There are times when co-parenting will not work and it should not even be tried. In families where a parent chronically abused his ex, it is unlikely that she can ever again find the trust required to co-parent effectively. Domestic abuse is likely not what you experienced as you and your ex fought your way toward divorce. Shouting, shoving, and even blocking your ex from leaving the room while you finished shouting what you had to say are certainly not commendable behaviors, but if they were infrequent, episodic losses of control in the heat of battle, then they do not constitute chronic domestic abuse. But actual domestic abuse, whether physical violence (your ex punches you and throws things at you) or emotional (your ex harasses you at work or monitors all your outside contacts, even your phone calls and email), causes permanent damage to you and your child, even if it leaves no lasting physical scars, and differs vastly from the fights typical in most divorces.

Similarly, where there are documented patterns of abuse toward a child, co-parenting cannot and must not be the path taken by parents or ordered by the court. Until psychotherapy helps effect a significant change in the parent's outlook and behavior, a child's contact with the abusive parent should be supervised and limited.

But as discussed in earlier chapters, you must be certain before limiting contact, that the behaviors are abusive and not just claimed as abusive for the sake of winning custody. Unfortunately, it is all too common in acrimonious custody battles to accuse your ex of abuse. He says, "She hits the child." However, in our society, spanking does not disqualify one from co-parenting. She accuses him of sexually molesting their child; there is no evidence, but she claims that he walked around the house undressed, exposing himself, and that she fears other, worse interactions may have occurred when her ex and child were alone together.

Accusations of child sexual abuse are difficult to resolve, as we saw with the family of Bob, Fran, and Sophia. Even after the police or the county's child protective services department discounts the accusation, trust has been shattered so significantly that co-parenting may not work.

Other situations may preclude co-parenting, too, but they are decided on a case-by-case basis. Some children and youth, like those with attachment disorders or bipolar disorder, are especially vulnerable and also very reactive to even a moderate level of stress. For these children, the transitions from one home to the other are less the issue than the conflicts that erupt when their co-parents argue over a decision. These vulnerable children can be so behaviorally and emotionally aggressive that co-parenting, with even appropriate levels of disagreement, is likely to cause the child so much anxiety that co-parenting may not be in the child's best interests.

Other children have mobility problems, chromosomal disorders, developmental delays, or injuries that make it too difficult to transition from one household to the other. The child may rely upon medical supportive devices that are too expensive to have in both households. Perhaps one parent is far more skilled than the other at the nursing care required for a particular child. But joint living arrangements and co-parenting are not synonymous. In order for children to thrive post-divorce, they need significant, ongoing relationships with both their co-parents. This does not mean that they must live with both co-parents. The quality of the relationship is not dictated by any particular living arrangement. Instead, the hallmark of successful co-parenting relies in these instances, as in most others, on the creativity of the co-parents to do what is best for their child.

Think About Co-Parenting, but . . .

Handicaps are not, however, unconditional deterrents to co-parenting. Physical impairments affecting daily life may certainly limit how co-parents are involved with their child, but they do not necessarily preclude the physically challenged parent from caring for and making decisions for the child. For example, I observed a situation where, after a stroke left one parent disabled and limited her mobility, she and her daughter maintained their close relationship through new activities and bonds. They read together, studied a foreign language together, and watched travel videos that took them vicariously to the places they could not visit in person. Meanwhile, the co-parents continued to consult regularly about their daughter's needs, and they made important decisions jointly.

Psychological and emotional handicaps also need not necessarily rule out effective co-parenting. Significant disorders like schizophrenia, bipolar syndromes and depression can all be treated and managed with psychotherapy and medication. Unless the psychological problem impairs the parent's judgment and imperils the children's safety, a co-parent's psychological illness does not in and of itself bar co-parenting.

The litmus test is: Does the disorder impact the ability of this parent to care for the child and make decisions? An actively hallucinating, schizophrenic parent who thinks his children are devils who must be destroyed endangers the children and is not only not fit to co-parent but must without a doubt be kept at a safe distance. But the schizophrenic parent who is stabilized thanks to treatment and medication and who can focus on the needs of the children can indeed co-parent, and the children will benefit from core relationships with both parents.

Even the seemingly most intractable and obtuse of mates can often be reconciled to act for the greater good of the child. While the breadth and intensity of the parental conflict before, during, and after divorce influences the likely outcome of co-parenting, co-parents can be taught, often with the help of a parent coordinator (and this book) how to remember their ex and their ex's interactions with their child in a different light. But when the conflicts were severe in the past and have not abated, when they revolved around different approaches to raising the child, when the past cannot be recast in a positive light, then effective co-parenting faces an uphill battle.

Yet not every divorce or parent coordination is a case from hell, although just about every judge, lawyer, pediatrician, or colleague who refers families to me characterizes the situation that way. All divorces involve powerful clashes and tensions as two people, once a couple, diverge from the life planned together into two separate, and, because they are unknown, somewhat frightening directions. Both suffer from the emotional upheavals and financial fallout of divorce. What is critical for co-parenting in the future is not the conflict itself but rather the resolution of the conflict, which allows the exes to go on with their lives and to raise their child together.

But when the conflict is so intense—that one-in-a-hundred case that really is from hell because the parents cannot let go of their rage—then co-parenting just will not work. At least, it will not work without some serious help.

Enter the parent coordinator.

Parent Coordination

Jesse and Anna were divorced far longer than they had been married. The divorce was contentious. Each asked for sole legal custody of their two young sons, Mark and Nick, then aged four and two-and-a-half, while they hurled a slew of accusations at each other. Jesse claimed Anna alienated the children from him; Anna pointed to Jesse's anger management problems. She accused him of being an alcoholic; he countered that she was sexually promiscuous and, consequently, morally unfit to mother his sons. As so often happens in venomous custody battles, Mark and Nick's grandparents on both sides fueled the acrimony and helped fund the fight. Jesse and Anna hired and fired several lawyers along the way; each new attorney came across as more combative than the last. What had been a loveless and disconnected but relatively unemotional marriage that had somehow produced two healthy and lovely boys now became a dangerous and deadly war zone.

As the fight over custody and equitable distribution went forward, legal fees soared and expenses for expert witnesses at the forthcoming trial loomed. With the financial costs of the divorce already far exceeding the parents' and grandparents' expectations, a few days before trial, Jesse and Anna finally agreed to joint legal custody, even though that agreement did not fully lay out how they would together arrange for the boys' medical care and education or how they would arrive at decisions about their sons' social, religious, extracurricular, and vacation activities. Given the boys' ages and Jesse's work schedule, Anna and Jesse agreed that Mark and Nick would spend most of their time with their mother but that they would stay with their father on alternate weekends and also spend one night a week at his home. Anna hoped that Jesse's interest in his young sons would soon wane.

Needless to say, Jesse and Anna's co-parenting got off to a rocky start. Each tried to set the young boys against the other co-parent. Before too long, Anna's expectation that Jesse would be little involved in her young sons' lives seemed to become a reality. Jesse began dating, and his contact with the boys decreased. They still visited him on alternate weekends, but sometimes the weekend started on Saturday afternoon rather than on Friday night. Now Jesse often skipped their midweek overnights. Jesse had said that he fought for his sons solely for their sake, to save them from the rigidity of his ex. But as new interests compelled his attention—his career, a new relationship, and eventually his remarriage—Jesse confided to friends, although never to his ex or the court, that, frankly, young children bored him. Consequently, over the next several years, Anna made most parenting decisions alone. Jesse showed up for some school events and pediatrician checkups, but otherwise he was absorbed in his career, his new wife, and their new daughter.

But as the boys grew old enough for team sports, Jesse became far more engaged with his sons. He enjoyed taking them to their games and practices on his alternate weekends. Then one year, when Mark's football coach became ill right before the season started, the team moms asked Jesse and another father to step in to coach. Jesse, who had always been a jock, agreed and loved his new role. He took coaching seriously, attended coaches' clinics, and spent time trolling the Internet for age-appropriate drills and activities for the team. In a short time Jesse had transitioned from an every-other-weekend parent watching his sons' games from the sidelines to a dedicated, even fanatically involved, parent and coach who not only found a football team for his younger son, Nick, but who also rearranged his work schedule so that he could help with his sons' midweek practices, too.

At first, Anna hesitantly welcomed Jesse's renewed interest in their sons' lives. She saw the boys thriving with their sports under their father's watchful eye. But soon Jesse ended up seeing the boys two evenings a week instead of the one prescribed in the custody agreement, because the boys practiced on different nights. A few times Anna became concerned that their practices interfered with homework, but, by and large, she and Jesse did not argue.

But the summer before Jesse began his second season as a coach, conflicts erupted anew. Jesse wanted his sons to have several weeks of intensive training that summer at a football camp. He had found one that boasted of the number of its graduates who went on to play college ball; at this camp, the boys would practice three times a day, get in-depth instruction, have outstanding coaching, and see close-up demonstrations by college players. Anna refused. She thought it was fine for the boys to spend a week of their summer at a local football clinic, but she didn't have the time, the money, or the desire to put them into a competitive summer program. That first summer she and Jesse compromised. While the boys were with her, they attended a local football camp for a week; then Jesse "used up" one of his two uninterrupted summer vacation weeks with Mark and Nick to send them to the football camp he had chosen.

But Anna was far from happy. Jesse, who had been uninvolved with his sons for so long, was now exceeding, with his coaching and his decision making about the boys' football, not only the parameters of what Anna had been accustomed to, but also the stipulations of their custody agreement. Moreover, Anna became increasingly agitated about the demands Jesse and his zeal for athletics were making on her family life.

He wanted the boys to work out daily and also to follow a strict diet: high-carbohydrate snacks before practice, a high-protein dinner afterward, no junk food, no quick frozen waffles or cold cereals for breakfast. When Anna picked them up from practice, Mark and Nick told her that they could no longer stop for fast food or pizza for dinner, because it was not healthy. After working all day and then driving the boys to practices and games, Anna was tired, did not have time to shop and cook, and certainly did not want to hear what her sons could and could not eat. Jesse also insisted that the boys not buy school lunches but rather that they or Anna should pack healthy lunches at home, which also meant that Anna was expected to keep their fridge well stocked.

When Anna discovered the boys skipping some of their homework in order to complete the daily exercise grids they had to fill out for their dad, she had had enough.

Anna and Jesse met at a coffee bar. She demanded that he stop denigrating her lifestyle in front of the boys and interfering with her parenting. Jesse countered by insisting that she was damaging them irrevocably because she did not buy rBGH-free milk or eggs laid by cage-free hens. Anna became infuriated and pulled out their original custody agreement, demanding that Jesse abide by it. Jesse unrelentingly insisted that Anna's obstinacy over the boys' diet and exercise plans endangered them and made her an abusive mother. Anna threatened to file contempt-of-court charges against Jesse for exceeding his allotted contact with the boys. Jesse threatened to file for sole legal and physical custody, insisting that he alone was concerned about his sons' health and welfare. After each accused the other of attempting to alienate their children, they stormed out of the meeting.

Then, without telling Anna, Jesse took the boys to try out for travel football teams and told Mark and Nick not to tell Anna, especially since there was no guarantee that they would make the teams. When they did, and when Anna found out from her two excited sons what was involved, she became enraged. Now each of the boys would practice four times during the week; weekend games and tournaments could be anywhere within a fifty-mile radius. The incursions into Anna's time and energies and also the added costs of this activity for a single working mother were far more than she could bear.

Just as Anna was trying to figure out how to respond to the news, an email from Jesse arrived. Jesse implied that the boys trying out for the travel teams had been a random, last-minute decision. Of course, he bragged about how much making the teams attested to the success of the training program he had designed for their sons. He then added that he was going to be assistant coach for Nick's team, and whenever he could, he would also help coach Mark's. He acknowledged the hardship and impact this might have on her schedule, then went on to offer as a solution that the boys spend the weekend nights at his house so they could be ready to go early on Saturday morning for their games, practices, and tournaments. "I am sure we can work out some other times when the boys can be with you to make up for these extra weekends with me," he added condescendingly.

Anna responded in turn: she would not consent to the boys playing in a travel football league, and she filed a contempt charge in court, claiming that Jesse was attempting to alienate her children from her and that he had broken the visitation schedule set by their original custody agreement. Jesse filed a counter-motion, asking the court to give him sole legal and physical custody of his sons. Before setting a court date, the judge ordered Anna and Jesse to meet with a parent coordinator.

Your legal custody agreement reads: "Parents agree it is in the best interests of their child to have the benefits of the wisdom and experience of both parents as active participants in his life. To that end, the parents agree to joint legal custody. All decisions of substance in the life of the child until the age of eighteen shall be made by both parents. The parents agree to share relevant information and desires and to reach jointly agreement about issues of substance or significance in the life of their child, including but not limited to the child's educational, medical, mental health, extracurricular, religious training, and summer activities and moral upbringing. The parents agree to work together toward making these decisions jointly in the best interests of the child."

That's the agreement. Then the reality hits. What happens when two people who can only glare at each other and cannot begin a conversation without "I told you so . . ." have to consider together their child's preschool admissions?

How do co-parents negotiate the very same disagreements about religion, morality, and ethical behavior that contributed to the breakup of the marriage as they continue to relate to the future of their child? How do the co-parents make rational decisions together when new circumstances renew their anger and pain? How do you agree on the child's summer plans when your ex's support check is late? How does your ex agree to accommodate your travel for work when you have married the man with whom you were having an affair that contributed to the breakup of your marriage? What happens when your ex just says no to what you perceive as a significant financial need for your child? What happens when a co-parent uses power over joint decisions to blackmail the other?

Your custody agreement reads that together both co-parents will make "all decisions of importance in the life of the child." But you cannot reach agreement, so you resort to the court once again. Let the court decide if a tutor—or a therapist or football camp—constitutes a "decision of importance" upon which both exes must agree.

Now you can see why the courts have become so overburdened when the only solution to these impasses is to return to the court to rule either on the specific point of contention or to make a change to the legal agreement.

But even if the court rules that this is a matter of importance requiring both co-parents' assent, you are already in court showing the judge that you and your ex cannot jointly decide. So you are asking the court to parent, to rule on whether or not your child needs that tutor or therapist or football camp. For years judges have made these rulings, but they must, because of their schedules and the legal process, limit their decision making to the single point in contention, one single motion.

Most court jurisdictions have a motion day where judges hear specific matters of previously decided cases. Generally, each motion gets a fifteen to thirty-minute hearing before the judge must move on to the next family.

One issue is decided, one battle ends, but it was just a skirmish. Hostilities will go on for many years unless the warring exes learn how to call a truce and co-parent together. Judges who rule on motions know they are seeing only the tip of the iceberg where these co-parents wage war. So they admonish the co-parents: "I don't want to see a matter like this again in my court. The two of you need to work these matters out in a manner that is best for your child." But how do the hostile co-parents do that? Generally they don't.

So they return to court once again. The judge has tired of these parents constantly using his courtroom to referee these decisions. The judge is also well aware that, unless these co-parents learn how to work together and make decisions for their child, they will return again. So the judge orders them to meet with a parent coordinator.

With more and more divorced families co-parenting their children over a decade or more, family courts, already overburdened, have recognized the need for parent coordinators when co-parenting doesn't work.

Parent coordination is a relatively new form of intervention for divorced couples fighting over how to raise their children. In the 1960s and 1970s, as most states enacted no-fault divorce laws (Utah, in 1984, was the last to do so), and with other societal changes underway, divorce rates skyrocketed and have remained high ever since. As of 2006, the United States had the highest divorce rate in the Western world. At the same time, with gender roles shifting, expectations for fathers, who in the past had been either stern patriarchs or distant breadwinners, have changed. They are now more prone to be intimately involved in the lives of their children from the delivery room forward. If and when these fathers divorce, they increasingly demand either sole legal custody of their children or concede grudgingly to joint legal custody and to co-parenting them.

Parent coordinators are either family law or mental health professionals who have considerable experience with high-conflict families. Although most states do not specifically license parent coordinators, you should look for one who affiliates with the professional Association of Family and Conciliation Courts and who also adheres to the guidelines for parent coordination established by the American Psychological Association. Parent coordinators do not become the co-parents' therapists. Instead, they have several mandates. First, they educate the warring exes about how to co-parent, build consensus, and compromise. Second, they help the parents implement their existing custody arrangements. Third, if the co-parents cannot agree, then the parent coordinator, who in some states might be officially designated master of the court, has authority from the court to make binding recommendations and decisions in the best interests of the child.

You may have encountered other mediators, custody evaluators, therapists, or guardians *ad litem* along your road to divorce. The parent coordinator differs from all of these. She becomes neither your nor your child's therapist, nor is she charged with discovering the truth behind the child's relationship with each of his parents and then reporting those findings to the court. Instead the parent coordinator, a highly skilled individual with expertise in child development and conflict resolution who has significant experience with how divorce and conflict affect the behavior and emotionality of children, works to train the co-parents to resolve their conflicts on their own and to make decisions in the best interests of their child. If the co-parents fail to agree, then the parent coordinator can often make binding decisions about child-rearing issues and also parental behavior.

In addition to focusing on compliance with your custody agreement, the parent coordinator starts from where you and your child are now. He makes decisions based on his expertise in understanding the developmental and emotional needs of your child at this moment in time. The effectiveness of the parent coordinator comes from his training in assessing the strengths and weaknesses of the parents and children, his understanding of child development and pathology, and his deep knowledge of the impact of divorce and conflict on the behavior and emotionality of children.

Parent coordinators can help exes who are co-parents work through issues that have arisen in the years since the divorce that the custody agreement did not explicitly lay out, and that a judge cannot possibly fully consider in a quarter hour. If you and your ex are arguing over your child playing softball because team practices interfere with your ex's night for visitation, then the parent coordinator will assess the needs of both co-parents and child, but the child's needs come first. If softball is integral to the child's sense of self and accomplishment and social life, then the parent coordinator must try to help the co-parents understand not only that they must reach agreement for the sake of their child—which, in theory, they know—but also that this fight perpetuates their old marital patterns of "beating up" on each other, and that this time another victim falls in the battle: their child.

If the co-parents cannot understand the child's needs, if they cannot compromise or reach an agreement, then the parent coordinator, authorized by the court, renders a decision. In some states, judges will deem that decision binding until a court of jurisdiction rules otherwise. In other states, parent coordinator decisions come in the form of recommendations taken under consideration by the court in future motions. Parent coordinators usually have wide discretion vis-à-vis custody agreements, as long as the decisions they make do not alter the essential structure of those agreements. In other words, if co-parents have joint legal custody, a parent coordinator cannot modify that to give one parent sole legal custody. In the case of the family in which the parents fought over softball practices, the parent coordinator could recommend that midweek visitation take place on another night, that it be temporarily eliminated to accommodate the child's practices, or that the time of weekend visitations with the co-parent who has lost contact hours with her child to softball be extended. Not only would the court endorse any of these rulings, but the judge would be relieved to know that an independent expert who fully understood the situation and the child's welfare had made the decision.

When can parent coordinators be helpful? When co-parents cannot understand that the agreement made for midweek visitations with Daddy when your daughter was eight and had no more than twenty minutes of homework a night no longer works for the adolescent with a full course load whose SAT prep course meets on the nights of Dad's visitation; when your ex remarries and plans to move, with your daughter, to follow her new husband and his job two thousand miles away; when one co-parent is consistently late for pickup and drop-off; when the other co-parent buys a house across town, and the driving arrangements you two had worked out so carefully fall apart. As mental health experts, parent coordinators can help co-parents deal with unanticipated medical and psychological problems and with alcohol and substance abuse. They can help parents who have absolutely no idea what goes on with their child when he is in the other co-parent's home communicate effectively about the child.

A parent coordinator will spend considerable time gaining an understanding of the needs of the child. Sometimes the parents will describe those needs; sometimes the parent coordinator will hear them directly from the child; sometimes he will hear from both. The parent coordinator then tries to reshape the problematic patterns of co-parent communication and behaviors that she understands as negatively impacting the child. The parent coordinator, while remaining the child's advocate in any given situation, tries to both teach the co-parents to view the conflict through their child's eyes and to also convince them to adopt a business model for negotiating with each other about their child. The parent coordinator teaches appropriate communication and advocates compromise and consensus with a focus on the present, not the past, to resolve conflicts until the co-parents learn to do this on their own.

Parent coordinators focus both on process and content. Process teaches the parents how to better communicate, how to assess the wants and needs of the child, and how to compromise and reach agreement. The parent coordinator will establish communication guidelines. When do the parents call each other? What goes into a text message?

How many emails should flow in a day? The coordinator helps the parents establish what appropriately belongs in a co-parenting email and what is a reasonable time for response. The coordinator develops guidelines for parental meetings and guides the parents in how to convey their decisions to the kids they love.

The focus on content deals with making the actual, hard decisions: your child will play baseball in Dad's neighborhood or soccer in Mom's, for example. Parent coordinators often help co-parents implement the terms of their court order. Your order may say, Dad has visitation with the kids every Wednesday evening for dinner. But it likely won't say whether Dad picks up the kids or you drop them off on your way home from work, what time dinner starts and ends, when homework gets done on Wednesday nights, and who is in charge of supervising the homework. If the co-parents cannot agree, the parent coordinator helps them fill in the details.

At first, the parent coordinator typically meets alone with each co-parent. The purpose of this individual meeting is to understand the history of the parental relationship and the parents' view of the child's needs. After that, most meetings will be with the two parents together. With some high-conflict families, I hold weekly parent coordination sessions. With other families, we meet once or twice a year to review potential schedule changes.

To get the most out of your parent coordinator, bring to the parent coordination meetings your process and specific content concerns. You can review what language should not be in emails between co-parents. You can also discuss issues you and your ex have been unable to resolve. You can discuss whether your child should be playing baseball, soccer, or both; whether your daughter needs a math tutor; who will drive your son to his weekly allergy shots.

13: BREAKING UP YOUR BREAKUP

The parent coordinator is neither your friend nor your adversary. She may sometimes agree with you and at other times disagree. Her job is to help you implement your court order, teach you strong co-parenting skills, and resolve parental conflicts for the benefit of the child. The parent coordinator is not your therapist, although he may recommend that a parent seek counseling if psychological issues interfere with effective co-parenting.

Parent coordinators teach new methods of co-parenting after divorce, establish guidelines for communication and transitions between the parents, and issue recommendations or directives when the parents cannot reach decisions. The parent coordinator becomes the advocate for the best interests of the child.

CHAPTER 14

Protecting Your Family Forever

Morgan and Charles were married many years before they decided to have a child. But once Courtney came along, what had once been a fun, open relationship with few responsibilities changed. Morgan began to feel Charles took her for granted. As he increasingly shied away from both housework and child care, she came to resent him even more. The intimacy of their relationship faded, and Morgan began a long-term affair with a married man at work who promised to leave his wife for her.

Morgan separated from Charles and filed for divorce. And although they lived in a no-fault divorce state, meaning no grounds were required for divorce, Morgan charged Charles with emotional and physical abuse. Charles countersued, charging Morgan with adultery. After six months of suits and countersuits, Morgan and Charles settled their case and agreed upon on a shared legal and physical custody of Courtney. Their divorce agreement ordered them into parent coordination.

During their first co-parenting session, Morgan and Charles agreed to a "business plan" that set guidelines for email and phone contacts for communicating about Courtney. However, two weeks later, in the second co-parenting session, Morgan dropped a bombshell when she announced she was four months pregnant with her boyfriend's child. But since he had decided to go back to his wife, Morgan told Charles she would be raising this child by herself.

Charles looked like a load of bricks had fallen on his head. He had a visceral, gut-wrenching reaction to the news that another man had impregnated his wife while she and he were still technically married. For the rest of the meeting, he kept staring at Morgan's slightly bulging stomach and muttering, "Why . . . why?"

The co-parenting arrangements fell apart. Charles refused Morgan permission to enter his apartment as Courtney switched from his residence to hers. He cut off all communications with Morgan and repeatedly told Courtney that her mother was a whore. He filed motions to change from joint to sole custody, arguing that his daughter should not be raised by a morally depraved mother, even though Charles had slept with other women after his separation. Finally the court forced him to return to co-parent counseling.

When Charles and Morgan returned to my office, he sat with his back to her and never addressed her directly. When he did glare at her, he directed his stare to her pregnant belly and moaned. He asked if the co-parenting meetings could be held individually or in separate rooms and wanted me, as the parent coordinator, to shuttle between them, like a State Department diplomat.

As Morgan's pregnancy advanced, Charles's rage grew. I warned him repeatedly about the impact of his behavior on his vulnerable daughter, and intellectually he understood the problem. However, he was emotionally ravaged, and he could not change. He refused to respond to emails or text messages from Morgan and continued to call her "you whore." Eventually Courtney became the State Department diplomat, shuttling between her parents to convey essential information like changes to her schedule. Soon she withdrew socially, and the A's and B's she had always gotten in school gave way to C's.

Meanwhile, Charles's rage went unchecked. Because the court order had not specified phone contact between Courtney's two homes, when she stayed with Charles he would not let her call her mother. Charles sent emails to the parents of Courtney's friends and softball teammates, raging about Morgan's immoral character. He even called the human relations department where she worked to draw their attention to her depravity. His attacks further depressed Morgan, who was already deflated by the pregnancy and the collapse of her relationship with her lover. Yet these two parents continued to share Courtney as she moved each week from one home to the other.

Even though the court order had prohibited Charles and Morgan from disparaging each other, Morgan dared not file contempt charges against Charles, since she knew she was guilty of failing to reveal her pregnancy during the divorce when the lawyers asked if there were any factors that could reasonably impact her co-parenting Courtney.

Meanwhile, I insisted that Charles enter individual psychotherapy for anger management. I arranged a joint meeting with Charles, his mother, Courtney's teacher, and the family pediatrician, an old friend of Charles. We all confronted him with the effect his anger had on Courtney. Charles got the message, and the outward displays of anger stopped. After Morgan gave birth, when Charles was no longer confronted with Morgan's visible manifestation of her "sin," his rage diminished to a degree, and an uncomfortable co-parenting arrangement was resumed.

Letting Go of Anger

After divorce, sometimes rage not only still runs high but may even intensify. That's because while you were married, you managed to overlook your ex's flaws. But now, as family and friends side with you, they join in a chorus denouncing your ex. For years your parents never said a bad word about your child's other parent. Now they have free rein to tell you, as if you did not already know, how selfish and stupid your ex is. Family and friends thus feed your rage.

At the same time, the legal process, with its battles over custody, property, and money and its demands for discovery, interrogatories, and depositions, also promotes and is driven by anger and fury. Yet it also has forbidden you to exhibit that anger.

When you and your ex exchange your child and he decides that is a good moment to share with you that he is dating his summer intern, you want to scream that your ex is a scuzzy, lowlife son of a bitch, but you have signed an agreement that reads, "You cannot degrade or allow degrading remarks to be made about each other, either in the presence of your children or in a fashion where your children could reasonably become aware of such." Your family and friends have given you permission to hate your ex, but you cannot display that rage in front of your child or you will be the one in trouble with the court.

When he admits that he propositioned the eighteen-year-old babysitter you spent weeks cultivating through the mommy network—explaining why she never sat for you again—you cannot say a word. But if you fail to give him a copy of Johnny's paper plate turkey made at school for Thanksgiving—even if, before the divorce, your ex did not know the name of Johnny's teacher or where his classroom was—you will be the one admonished and held in contempt of court, because the court has ordered you to "convey all appropriate educational information in a timely fashion, in a manner that is comprehensive and that appropriately conveys educational reports, data, programming, progress, special events, grades, and copies of all other work products that a reasonable person would wish to have."

14: PROTECTING YOUR FAMILY FOREVER

Anger is a dominant theme in separation, divorce, and co-parenting. The families I generally see, the cases that proceed either to full-blown custody evaluations or court-ordered parent coordination, are always toxic. To repair the relationships essential for successful co-parenting in these cases is difficult and takes much time.

Divorce and anger go together—you won't have one without the other. But after reminding yourselves of that basic co-parenting principle of reducing conflict, you realize that you will need to channel anger against your ex elsewhere so that you can manage a relationship with your ex and your child. You do not want your child, who was already exposed to so much anger while you were married and separating, living with any more of it after you have divorced.

But how do you do that when the divorce has challenged your identity as a married family person, damaged your financial security, likely mandated a move away from the home and neighborhood you have lived in for so many years, and perhaps even shattered your self-image? It has challenged old loyalties and friendships as your friends have chosen between you and your ex, and it has also polarized your children between you and your former spouse.

All that frustration and that rage then carries over into the co-parenting relationship, as it did for Morgan and Charles. So how on earth do you actually pull off controlling your anger for the rest of time, or at least until your child is out on her own? What do you do with all that rage?

You tell your friends. That's what friends are for. To effectively co-parent, you certainly have to discharge your anger. But you must do it away from your child and in such a way that your child is unlikely to find out about it. Certainly, some raging parents will need, as Charles did, psychotherapy to learn how to deal with their anger. Even when Charles intellectually understood how calling his daughter's mother a whore hurt his child, he could not manage, without therapy, to curb his temper. But most others will find a friend to listen to their complaints and help them deal with their anger. Later, one hopes, that friend will also help you move forward to let go of that anger.

The ground rule here is that the child must be protected from the ravages of rage. Your child cannot—must not—be allowed to live in an environment of anger where one parent maligns the other. The level of conflict post-divorce is a key factor impacting the emotional, social, academic, and behavioral outcomes for your child. If the angry co-parent cannot learn to displace rage effectively, co-parenting will fail. And the individual who is damaged most will be your child.

Good Parenting, Even When You Disagree

In a marriage, most couples make a deal, whether explicitly or implicitly. One might follow a furious career track with its financial rewards, but its downside is a lot of travel. The other finds a job that allows him to pick up the child on time from after-school care. Or the parents coordinate their schedules so that when one is crunched at work, the other handles the pediatrician and school appointments. After all, someone has to cover the 185 days a year when the child is not in school.

But divorce breaks these deals. When you divorce, the old arrangements fall by the wayside. And the agreed partnership about who made the money and who did the child rearing is now irrelevant. Now each parent wants to be recognized as the primary parent with greater rights and responsibilities over their child than the other.

She will claim she has that right because she spent more time raising him. She will argue, with validity, the value of all those years of experience. She knows the difference between a real virus and lazy malingering, between a social slight and bullying, between laziness and learning problems, between a real nightmare and your child just needing a hug.

He will counter: "But I love my child, too." And he can chronicle his contributions to raising the child as well: all the times he woke the child to make sure he got ready for school on time, all those baths and bedtime stories, the Saturday trips to the hardware store, and the fun of watching Sunday football games together. All these prove, so he asserts with validity, his competency as a father.

She disagrees. Sure, her ex spent time with the child, but mostly under her supervision and guidance. He knows next to nothing about what it takes to raise a child when she's not around. He had nothing to do with toilet training; he got frustrated when your child struck out at bat with bases loaded; he made your daughter cry when he brought home orange balloons for her birthday, because he did not know that her favorite color was pink; and the one time you went out of town with your girlfriends, he fed the kid frozen food and McDonald's for three straight days. Your ex cannot possibly raise your child properly. His time with her must be limited for the sake of your child.

But child-rearing skills are not innate, and they can, with time, be learned. For some parents they come naturally, while for others they do not. If you spent ten years raising your child and he spent ten years programming computer systems, is it fair to test him on child rearing—or you on computer programming—without giving him or you education, training, and experience in the field? Who now has knowledge of the child's behavioral and emotional needs and nuances may be less important for future co-parenting than who can learn these skills. You argue that waiting for your ex's learning curve to kick in is not in your child's best interests. I argue that what counts now is the child's welfare and understanding the child's behavioral and emotional needs. A good father and a good mother, who teach, model, wield parental authority judiciously, and provide structure and discipline—they are the basic component of good parenting. But the paths they take can vary widely.

The two adults need not parent in the same way, and both must realize that. Instead, what is vital for your child's future growth and development is a positive and meaningful relationship with each parent well into the future and the elimination of conflict between the co-parents. Though feeding your child fast-food hamburgers and playing video games with him may not be your idea of good parenting, they do not, in and of themselves, make one parent inadequate. In fact, these activities, which you see as not in your child's best interests, afford moments for important parent-child interactions. You and your child sit down to a well-balanced meal at 6:30 every night. But your ex cannot do that; he never learned how to cook, and he does not have the time. What is meaningful to your child is that she and one of her co-parents eat together every night. The setting and what she eats do not leave a lasting impression; what leaves an impression is that dinner times were parent times.

You want your child in bed by 9:30; your ex puts him to bed after 10:00. Do you really think your child will be harmed by the difference? Will drinking organic milk in one house and not in the other affect the child? The answer is no, not so long as both parents learn to accept that now that they live apart, they are going to differ in how they raise their child. Don't allow those differences to be the source of greater and more destructive conflicts and disagreements. Of course your child may whine that you don't let him play video games and Dad does, but as with other childhood complaints, this is surely manageable.

Your child can get as much from watching a movie with one parent as playing catch with the other in the backyard. One parent likes to arrange playdates; the other spends Saturday afternoons baking cookies with his child. One parent allows more computer time, the other less. The differences in parenting styles are far less important than the co-parents accepting that their child will integrate aspects from both of them into her future development.

Your ex never was and never will be just like you. Your child can successfully learn from both of you, and you can both be good parents, even though your styles of parenting differ. It really does not matter whether or not your child eats a salad with his dinner or if dinner comes out of the freezer and goes into the microwave. What matters is that you and your ex avoid arguing over what you feed your child. Your ex will not parent the same way you do. Accept that for the sake of your child you love.

A Better Parent After the Divorce

Sondra and Stanley had high-powered careers. They had sacrificed personal lives while each had climbed the Washington, DC, political ladder. Sondra had held appointments in several federal administrations. Stanley had parlayed a military career into a very successful consulting business. They married as both approached forty. By then, Stanley was making considerable money as a consultant. But, as the administrations changed, Sondra, knowing that she would have to leave her current position as a political appointee and find a new, less demanding job, thought this a good moment to have a child. Stanley agreed.

When Sondra was pregnant, she and Stanley had discussed sharing child-rearing responsibilities. But once Julia was born, Stanley showed no interest in diapers or infancy playgroups. Sondra fell into the maternal role easily and shouldered the majority of Julia's care. Stanley remained responsible for overseeing his daughter's pediatrician appointments.

Sondra was a good mother. She bought the right toys, found a nanny, researched neighborhood preschools, and juggled quite successfully the demands of life as a career mom. Stanley was a more distant parent. He occasionally attended Julia's preschool interviews but, if asked, could not name his daughter's favorite color, food, or dress.

When Julia was four, they separated amicably because each was having an affair. They disagreed, however, when it came time to decide about Julia's custody. Sondra argued against co-parenting. She claimed that not only had she done the heavy lifting of parenting until now, but also that Stanley was "clueless" about how to raise a child.

In fact, both statements were true. Stanley, who had graduated with honors from a service academy and had rapidly ascended through the military ranks, failed all of the child development tests he took. He could not name his daughter's preschool teacher. He did not know the last name of her best friend. When asked about how he would deal with typical child development matters, like handling a temper tantrum or the child who wets the bed, Stanley displayed little knowledge or flexibility.

On the other hand, Sondra was an obviously excellent mother who had made herself practically an expert on child rearing. Before Julia was born, she had read a slew of child development books and could even point out discrepancies in their approaches. She had researched the educational philosophies of her local public and private schools. She knew a great deal about the latest health care concerns for preschoolers. She had put great time and energy, perhaps almost obsessively, into acquiring the skill set she needed to parent effectively.

Sondra clearly demonstrated the attributes of successful parenting; Stanley displayed none. Sondra argued therefore that Stanley should have only weekend daytime visitation with his daughter. Julia should not sleep at his house. Since he had almost never bathed her in the past and only rarely put her to bed, how could he, as a single parent, possibly care for his daughter during overnights?

Stanley agreed with Sondra that indeed she had done most of the parenting for their daughter. But, he explained, that was because they had agreed upon that arrangement. Stanley had also done heavy lifting for the family, but his was financial. As long as Sondra's political party was out of power, her position and income were limited. Had her party stayed in power and she remained in her old job, he would have been Julia's chief parent, and Sondra would have been the major breadwinner. He argued persuasively that it was unfair to punish him now for how he and Sondra had deliberately divided up the responsibilities of family life when they were married. He was also convinced that he could learn to become just as good a parent as Sondra. He was confident that not only could he acquire the skills he needed but also that he could adjust his lifestyle to co-parent his daughter.

Unfortunately, Stanley's first efforts to demonstrate his competency as a co-parent were not very successful. Not only did he come late to his daughter's preschool winter pageant, but her teacher had to ask him to turn his Blackberry off during the show. He made an appointment for his daughter's annual physical and immunizations, but Sondra had already taken her three weeks before. He once left his daughter alone at the McDonald's playground—just for a few minutes—because he had to take a call that required privacy.

Nevertheless, true to his word, Stanley indeed began to "get it." Whether prompted by his anger at Sondra and his refusal to allow her to show him up, by coaching from his therapist or lawyer, or just by his desire to be there to see his charming four-year-old grow up, Stanley began pouring his considerable intellect and energy into learning how to parent.

He read lots of books, took parenting classes, and even completed an online child development course. And it eventually worked. He worked hard to become a dependable, knowledgeable, and committed father. It took Sondra some time to acknowledge her ex's growth and change, but eventually she did. She and Stanley then agreed upon Julia's custody. They would jointly make decisions; Julia would have her primary residence with Sondra, but she would have gradually increasing overnight visitation times with her father.

Stanley's story proves that one can indeed learn to parent. During the marriage, one parent's involvement in the child's life may have been limited or lacking. Post-divorce, things can often change in very unexpected ways. Appropriate parenting skills can be learned.

What may come instinctually to some can, for the most part, be taught to those who do not naturally have the necessary skill set. Even if, while you were married, your spouse was mostly an absent parent, even if he never understood how to make a game for your preschooler out of picking up his toys, even if he never helped your sixth-grader with his science fair projects, your ex can, as Stanley did, learn how to be a competent parent. If your ex puts in the time and effort to do so, then together you can co-parent the child you both love so much. And you should give your ex and your child the opportunity to make that a reality.

You Are Still a Family

Les and Deborah had had a bitter divorce, but both loved their daughter, Emily, and so they tried to co-parent. Emily switched homes every other week, living one week with Deborah and the other with Les. But the parents' rancor toward each other never diminished, even after both remarried and acquired stepchildren. They reticently struggled to make decisions together until Emily graduated from high school.

14: PROTECTING YOUR FAMILY FOREVER

Everyone, including Emily, knew that when they invited both Les and his wife and Deborah and her husband anywhere they would not attend at the same time, because they could not bear to be in the same room with each other.

As Emily finally went off to college and then to graduate school, Les and Deborah completely stopped all contact with the other, even though Emily maintained relationships with both.

Years later Emily, now married and with children of her own, was giving a speech out of town. She shared the good news with both her parents, but never expected them to attend. She was quite surprised when they both showed up. But her father, Les, was even more surprised at the reception following the presentation when a woman approached and asked, "Do you know who I am?" Before he could reply, "No, we have never met," his second wife calmly interjected, "How are you, Deborah?"

Les and Deborah are the perfect example of what not to do. But there are countless other examples of a better way forward for you and your family: of divorced spouses who co-parented successfully and went on to celebrate together their children's graduations, weddings, and births of grandchildren. They shared the good times of the next stage of their lives—and the sad ones. They managed to put the past behind them and smile for the blended family photos for the sake of the child they loved and raised together, and especially for the grandchildren they both adored. Occasionally, all four—two co-parents and two stepparents, all of whom had traveled a long distance to celebrate a milestone with that child—stay in the same home. Other times, they gather together for an extended family reunion. I even know of one family in which a child's father and stepfather, who got along because both liked baseball, wanted to give their grown son a gift just before college graduation—all three went down to Florida for spring training.

Divorce does not end your relationship with your ex. Co-parenting took it to a new stage; when your child becomes an adult, you and your ex enter into yet another stage of your triangular relationship with your child.

Having a child binds you and your ex for life. The custody agreement you made when you were in your thirties lives on for years. When your child turns eighteen and is legally an adult, the court will bow out of your lives. Perhaps your custody agreement had a single sentence about how you two were going to pay for college, but beyond that, you, your ex, and your child move into uncharted territory. However, your triangular relationship continues. Your child will graduate from high school and college, get an apartment, get married, buy a house, have children, and start a new cycle of life's events. Both you and your ex, whether you co-parented successfully or not, will want to be there, to share in your child's life in the decades ahead. How you and your ex manage to co-parent your child to maturity will influence your time with your children and their new families in the years to come. If you don't work to keep your family together, then do not be surprised when it falls apart.

The decisions you make co-parenting will impact your children throughout their lives. Your child's perception that his mother and his father cannot be together for his wedding a quarter century after you two split will shape a new generation of damaged relationships. The modeling effect of two adults who once loved each other enough to wed but who could not put aside their animosity post-divorce for the sake of their children severely impacts the ability of those children to trust in their own relationships.

Imagine the arguments between your child and his fiancée about their wedding plans when your son explains why they cannot have the

14: PROTECTING YOUR FAMILY FOREVER

big wedding she has always dreamed of—because his parents can't stand the sight of each other.

Do you want your unborn grandson to worry about which grandparents can come to kindergarten on grandparents' visiting day? Do you want your daughter for the rest of her life to have to juggle the two of you for family events, inviting Mom to come to her child's birthday party at 1:00, and making certain she leaves by 2:15, just before Dad waltzes in at 2:30? Do you really want your four-year-old grandchild to learn that Grandma and Grandpa hate each other so much that they cannot be together for Christmas?

When your grandchildren hear these messages, you will have, yet again, broken a child's trust. Your grandchild—like her parent before her—now has to puzzle out the knowledge of her grandparents' inability to solve problems and relate to each other.

Your failure to co-parent successfully echoes across the generations, damaging this time not just your child but also your grandchild. If you and your ex cannot learn to deal with each other as you co-parent your own children, your unborn grandchildren, who you will love as fiercely as you love your child, will also suffer.

For the sake of your child, and for you and your family, learn to effectively parent the child you love with the ex you hate.

ACKNOWLEDGMENTS

First and foremost, I have to acknowledge that the stories I tell and the lessons I've learned do not belong to me. Behind the anecdotes and the pseudonyms are very real parents raising their kids with real love. I am indebted to these families, my patients, for courageously unfolding and sharing their lives with me. Their experiences, the successes and mishaps of parenting, shaped this book.

Greenleaf Book Group made this project a reality. My "handler," Hobbs Allison, and Jessica Marpe organized a team of professionals to shape the manuscript. Chris Benguhe, a gifted writer, retained the voice of my patients while developing a unifying theme. Linda O'Doughda, Thom Lemmons, and Patricia Fogarty were thoughtful and creative editors and Brian Phillips's artistic talents are evident in the cover design and layout. Bryan Carroll, Kris Pauls, and Steve Elizalde firmly moved the project along with grace and made sure the book got in the right hands at the right time.

The encouragement of my colleagues and staff at Reston Psychological Center is much appreciated. Dr. Arnold Small has been my expert go-to consultant for difficult clinical matters for the years we've been in practice together. Ms. Gloria Chemiel and Ms. Renee Mullen have supported me and the creation of this work with patience and good humor. The countless psychologists and attorneys with whom I've shared these experiences have been wonderful teachers.

My friends have humored me, challenged me, and supported me throughout this endeavor and I thank them all. But most importantly, I thank Dr. Norman Gold and Dr. Carol Weissbrod who allowed me to hole up in their beautiful Maine house to complete this manuscript.

My mother, Mrs. Sylvia Farber, has lovingly devoted her life to her children and family. At age ninety, she sharpened her number-two pencils and carefully edited the manuscript, finding typographical errors and misspellings that editors and computer software missed. Her meaningful daily support of this project and her love are inspirational.

Saving the most important for last, I thank the family I love. My wife, Dr. Pamela Nadell, is an accomplished academic, lecturer, community leader, and the author of many scholarly books that have significantly impacted our culture. She has shared this project with me as we have shared our lives, with compassion and dedication. Her brilliant conceptual and editorial skills are evident in every paragraph of this book. Her love is evident in every line of our lives. Our children, Yoni and Orly are the "Kids You Love," successful and strong young adults. Their dreams sustain me. It is to them that I dedicate this book with love.

INDEX

A

abuse
    emotional abuse, 104
    physical abuse of partner, 163, 164, 167–68
    See also child abuse
adolescents, 145–54
    changing needs, desires, and expectations, 136–40, 181
    with driver's license, 139–40, 151
    entering into the life of, 137–38, 139–41, 143
    rebellion against visitation schedule, 135–37
    right to some control, 139, 141–42, 143
    social calendars and visitation, 134–35, 138–40
    visitation examples, 133–35, 137–38, 148–50
    wanting to live with the other parent, 148–52
agreements. *See* co-parenting agreement; custody agreement
alcoholic parent, 125–27, 163–65, 181
alimony, 48
American Psychological Association guidelines for parent coordinators, 178
anger, letting go of, 187–90
anger management counseling for parents, 18, 187, 189–90
Association of Family and Conciliation Courts, 178

B

bar mitzvah controversy, 73, 74–75
bipolar disorder, 16–18, 116
birthday parties, 58–62, 87, 191, 199
birthday presents, 84
blame and blaming
    leaving child out of, 34–35
    preventing child from blaming herself, 37–38, 40, 159–60
borderline personality disorder, 116–18, 119–20
both parents. *See* relationship of child with both parents
braces, decision about, 28
bully exes, 105–13
    court as defense against, 109–11
    example of, 105–9
    fighting back, 111–13
business model
    child as priority, 75–76, 127–28
    child benefiting from, 24
    financial expectations clearly established, 49–51
    informing ex of a new partner in your life, 85
    learning from parent coordinator, 181, 185–86
    overview, 4, 24
    and special events, 55–56, 57

C

camp
    decision about attending, 28, 173–74, 177

as summer entertainment during long
visits, 3, 137
child abuse, 97–104
accusations of sexual abuse, 97–102, 168
Munchausen Syndrome by Proxy as, 121
potential ramifications, 102–3
reporting, 104
as sufficient cause to disallow parenting, 168
children, 155–60
breaking primary trust of, 32–33, 84, 158–59
developing their own opinions, 20–21
exaggerations of, 155–57
fantasizing about reuniting their parents, 40–41, 60, 83–84, 159
with mental or physical disorders, 168–69
needs, desires, and expectations, 136–40, 158–60
perception of relationship with both parents, 18–20, 158
perceptions of visitations, 155–60
perspective on divorce, 25–26, 32–33
physical necessities, 27–28
and presents for birthdays and holidays, 62
protecting from the ravages of rage, 190
school as stability during a divorce, 66–68
similarity to "bad" parent, 34–35
and stepparents, 93–95
telling you what you want to hear, 75, 87–88, 159–60
threat of parent's new relationship, 84–85
time, amount of, spent with each parent, 14
See also adolescents; counseling for child; relationship of child with both parents

children acting out their pain
child doesn't want to go to visitations, 22–23, 32, 134–35
complaining about the other parent, 46
and court-ordered visitation, 22–24
grades plummet, 16, 17, 24
illness as, 22–24, 46
mom complains about soccer coaching by dad, 54
new boyfriend or girlfriend, 84–85
self-sabotage with parents fighting, 53–55
son upset that mom interferes with visitation, 148
teens accused of borderline personality disorder, 117–19
telling each parent what they want to hear, 75, 87–88, 159–60
withdrawal, 107
children and divorce
child's exhaustion with the drama, 136, 141
child's need to NOT know details, 34–35
child's perspective of divorce, 25–26, 37–40
child's worries about offending a parent, 15, 17, 18, 54
overview, 5, 11–13, 190
parents' inability to acknowledge pain they are causing, 24
telling your child about the divorce, 37–42
child support
emotional aspects of receiving the check, 49
emotional aspects of writing the check, 48–49, 51
grandparents' sabotage, 45–47
overview, 48
Christmas, 58, 61–63
church, decision about, 28
clothing, decision about, 27–28

INDEX

communication with your child, 31–43
    informing your child of the divorce, 33, 37–42
    introducing a new partner, 86–87
    long distance relationships, 6–7
    telling about the divorce, 37–42
    telling ugly truths, 31–32
    timing and place for, 35–37
communication with your ex
    and children's exaggerations, 155–58
    child's honesty/safety as byproduct of, 29, 49, 158, 160
    and process aspect of parent coordination, 181–82, 183
    software program for logging, 50
    See also business model; decision-making process
conflict reduction
    and interpretation of your child's stories, 155–58
    letting go of your anger, 189–90
    overview, 15, 21–26
content aspect of parent coordination, 182
co-parenting
    accepting differences in style, 191–93
    accepting ex's issues, 27–28, 128
    binding nature of, 198–99
    creating two households for your child, 41–43
    and details of child's life, 27–28, 41–42
    financial expectations clearly established, 49–51
    grandparents' sabotage, 45–47, 74–75, 171
    and handicap of partner, 169–71
    initial stages, 40–43
    overreacting to child's comments about other parent, 155–58, 160
    overview, 13–15
    speak no evil about your ex, 18–21, 91, 167
    and stepparents, 90–91
    supporting visitation, 142–43
    time off for social life, 83
    validity of parents' claims to primary position, 190–91
    See also business model; conflict reduction; decision-making process; parenting; relationship of child with both parents
co-parenting agreement
    broadness of, 28–29
    on conveying educational information, 188
    on degrading remarks, 188
    mom with mental issues must take her medication, 123–24
    shiftless dad wants more time with son, 146–47
    See also custody agreement
co-parenting examples, successful
    mother as primary, father participating, 1–3, 6–8, 133–34
    overview, 197–98
    parents agree to be agreeable, 45, 47
    religious differences, 75–76
    shiftless dad wants more time with his son, 146–50
    unskilled dad learns how to parent, 193–96
    See also love and caring
co-parenting examples, unsuccessful
    accusations of child sexual abuse, 97–102, 168
    court-based decision making, 21–23, 26
    father cheating, mother bitter, 16–18
    grandparents' sabotage, 45–47, 74–75, 171
    joint legal custody, 105–9
    Munchausen Syndrome by Proxy example, 115–22
    out-of-control rage affecting child, 185–87
    religious differences, 73–75
    shiftless dad wants more time with

his son, 146–50
soccer coaching by dad leads to excessive visits complaint, 53–55
telling ugly "truths" to the child, 31–32
See also hate and warring
co-parenting, lack of capacity for
alcoholic parent, 125–27, 163–65, 181
dysfunctional relationship can't be overcome, 166
effects of, 198–99
mental issues, 123–24, 166
See also abuse; parent coordinator/coordination
counseling for child
children opening up in, 37–38
ex says no to, 107
mom's need to be justified, 118
result of sexual abuse accusation, 99–101, 102
counseling for parents
anger management, 18, 187, 189–90
substance abuse treatment program, 165
See also parent coordinator/coordination
court
decision making by, 21–23, 26, 177
for ex's bullying ploys, 111–12
motions day, 26, 177
court orders
bully's utilization of, 107–9
child ordered to go to scheduled visitations, 18, 22–23
mediation, 148–49
for parent coordination, 109, 112, 120, 124, 176–78
parent coordinator's help with, 182, 183
psychological evaluation of child, 17–18
substance abuse treatment, 165
violations of, 53, 187
custody agreement

conflicting points, 74–75
modifications to, 140
overview, 11–13, 176–77
on relationships with potential partners, 16–17, 82
and telling your ex about your new partner, 85
time, amount of, spent with each parent, 14–15
vagueness of, 177
war over exceeding stipulations of, 174–76
See also co-parenting agreement; schedule
custody evaluation, 123, 189

D

decision-making process
court-based decisions, 21–23, 26, 177
and court order, 28
face-to-face co-parenting discussions, 89–91, 174–75
overview, 15, 26–29
parents working together, 28–29
See also communication with your ex
depression, 124–25
discipline and stepparents, 94
divorce
accepting your ex, 19, 20, 27–28
breaking a child's primary trust, 32–33, 158–59
creating two households for your child, 41–43
cutting your ex out of your life, 21–23, 196–97
effects on partners, 121–22, 190
informing your child of, 33, 37–42
monetary costs, 47–48
no-fault divorce laws, 178
school as stability for your child, 66–68
time and place for conversation about, 35–37
See also children and divorce

E

emotional abuse, 104
emotions
    about child support, 48–49, 51
    allowing, 39
    entering into your child's life, 137–38, 139–41, 143
    events. *See* significant events
    exaggerations of children, 155–57

F

faith, decision about, 28, 72–76
fantasy about parents reuniting, 40–41, 60, 83–84, 159
financial expectations, 49–51
flexibility of parents, 1–3, 6–8, 63, 137–38, 140. *See also* co-parenting examples, successful

G

gender role shifts, 178
grandparents' sabotage, 45–47, 74–75, 171
grandparent visitation rights, 45, 46

H

handicap of partner, 169–71
hate and warring
    cutting your ex out of your life, 21–23, 196–97
    dysfunctional relationship can't be overcome, 166
    effects on child, 15, 21–24
    explosion moment, 147–48
    grandparents' sabotage, 45–47, 74–75, 171
    letting go of anger, 187–90
    mom pregnant by her lover before divorce is final; dad enraged, 185–87
    out-of-control rage affecting child, 185–87
    over exceeding stipulations of custody agreement, 174–76
    overview, 4, 5
    suppressing, for your child, 20–21
    See also co-parenting examples, unsuccessful
holidays, 58–63
home schooling, 70
honesty without cruelty, 32–33

J

joint legal custody
    bully ex, 111–13
    contentious parents agree to, 172–77
    effects of, 109–11
    example, 105–9
    sole custody vs., 166–67
    See also co-parenting

L

lawyers and child abuse accusations, 98–100, 103
learning disabilities, 69
love and caring, 8. *See also* co-parenting examples, successful

M

marriage
    child's fantasizing about reuniting parents, 40–41, 60, 83–84, 159
    conflict during, 24–25, 36
    to new partner, 91–95
mental issues, children with, 168–69. *See also* psychological problems of ex
money issues, 45–51
motions day at court, 26, 177
Munchausen Syndrome by Proxy, 115–22

N

neutral territory, school as, 71–72
new partners, 79–95
    and child's fantasy of reconciliation, 83–84
    dating, 81–83
    introducing your child, 86–88
    marriage to, 91–95
    sleepovers, 16–18, 80–81, 88–89
    telling your ex, 85
    threat to your child, 84–85

O

Our Family Wizard software, 50

P

parent coordinator/coordination, 171–83
    court order for, 109, 112, 120, 124, 176–78
    for financial plan development, 49
    mandates and power of, 178–80
    meetings with parents, 182–83
    mom pregnant by her lover before divorce is final; dad enraged, 185–87
    mom with psychological disorder, 116, 124
    overview, 170–71, 178, 181–82, 183
    situation leading to, 171–76
    soccer game attendance, 54–55
parenting
    comforting your child, 36
    entering into your child's life, 137–38, 139–41, 143
    flexibility required for, 1–3, 6–8, 63, 137–38, 140
    learning appropriate skills, 194–96
    letting your teenager live with other parent as, 152–53
    long-distance dad and son's homework, 2–3
    modeling good behavior, 124
    seeing conflict through your child's eyes, 181
    See also co-parenting
personality disorders, 127–28. *See also* psychological problems
physical handicap of partner, 169–70
post-transition adjustments, 61
preparation phase of transition, 60–61
presents for birthdays and holidays, importance of, 62
primary trust, 32–33, 84, 158–59
process aspect of parent coordination, 181–82
psychological evaluation of child
    for allegations of sexual abuse, 99–100
    court-ordered, 17–18
    mom with Munchausen Syndrome by Proxy takes her kids to multiple psychologists, 117, 118
    pediatrician referral refused by one parent, 107
psychological problems of child, 168–69
psychological problems of ex, 115–29
    alcoholic parent, 125–27
    mom with Munchausen Syndrome by Proxy example, 115–22
    parents with, 123–24, 166, 170
    personality disorders, 127–28
    schizophrenic mom controlled by medications, 122–24

R

rebound relationships, 81
relationship of child with both parents, 16–21
    alcoholic parent, 127, 165
    and holiday schedule, 58, 60–63
    importance of child's perception of, 18–21, 158
    negative example, 16–18
    overview, 14–15, 129, 191–93
    positive examples, 1–3, 6–8, 28–29
    See also co-parenting examples, successful; co-parenting examples, unsuccessful
relationships, new. *See* new partners
religious upbringing, decision about, 28, 72–76

S

schedule
    adolescents' right to some control, 141–42
    and adolescents' social calendars, 134–35, 138–40
    child's rebellion against, 135–37
    choosing a living arrangement, 14–15
    for holidays, 58, 60–63
    software programs for managing funds and, 50

and telling your child about the divorce, 39–40
    timing for discussion of, 57–58
schizophrenia, 122–24
school, 65–72
    choosing, 68–70
    father tries to change teenage daughter's school, 65–66
    home schooling, 70
    keeping child in the same school, 66–68
    overview, 72
    parental adjustment to, 70–72
    special events at, 71–72
    volunteering at your child's school, 70–71
sexual abuse, accusations of, 97–102, 168
significant events, 53–63
    birthday parties, 58–62, 87, 191, 199
    holidays, 58–63
    special school events, 71–72
    sports games, 55–58
sleepovers with new partner, 16–18, 80–81, 88–89
software programs for managing funds and schedule, 50
sole custody, 166–67
special events. *See* significant events
sports
    as bullying dad's way to cause problems, 108–9
    dad's coaching violates visitation privileges, 53–55
    dad's interest in children when old enough for, 172–76
    importance to child, 148, 180
spousal support, 48
stepparents, 89–95
substance abuse problems, 125–27, 163–65, 181
supervision of visitations, 101–2, 103

T

teenagers. *See* adolescents
time, amount of, spent with each parent, 14
time and place for introducing a new partner, 86–87
transitions from one home to the other
    children with mental or physical disorders, 168–69
    and holiday splitting, 60–63
    making children suffer and videotaping, 21–23
transitions from one school to another, 68, 72
trust (financial) for children, 50–51
tutoring, decision about, 28

V

visitations, 133–43
    adolescent example, 133–35, 137–38, 148–50
    with alcoholic parent, 126–27
    child doesn't want to go, 22–23, 32, 134–35
    children's perceptions of, 155–60
    and child's activities, 53–55
    child's needs as priority, 180–81
    details of, 182
    earning the right to, 194–96
    ex skipping opportunities, 172
    ex's disparaging remarks about, 21, 22
    ex's new partner's sleepovers, 16–18, 80–81, 88–89
    grandparent visitation rights, 45, 46
    with irresponsible parent, 146–48
    long distances, 2–3, 7
    other partner's judgment of, 19–21
    overview, 12
    responsibility for transporting the child, 106
    and sole custody, 166–67
    and stepparents, 92
    supervision of, 101–2, 103
    See also schedule
volunteering
    at child's school, 70–72
    as sports team coach, 53–55, 70–71, 173–76

ABOUT THE AUTHOR

Dr. Edward Farber is a licensed clinical psychologist in Virginia and Maryland. He is on the clinical faculty at the George Washington University School of Medicine and is the former chair of psychology at the Ohio State University Pediatrics Department and Nationwide Columbus Children's Hospital.

Recognizing the need for specialized services for families in transition or divorce, Dr. Farber founded Reston Psychological Center and Reston Family Center to provide pre-divorce counseling, custody evaluations, visitation assessments, parent coordination interventions, psychological assessments, and psychotherapy. Dr. Farber has published professionally, lectured nationally, and received multiple research grants. He has served on several national and local community boards. Dr. Farber has treated hundreds of families of separation and divorce and has been recognized by his colleagues as a top therapist in the *Washingtonian* magazine. Dr. Farber lives in the Washington, DC, area with his wife and children.

www.ingramcontent.com/pod-product-compliance
Lightning Source LLC
Chambersburg PA
CBHW060521080526
44586CB00012B/563